HANOCH LEVIN: SELECTED PLAYS TWO

Hanoch Levin

SELECTED PLAYS TWO

Suitcase Packers
The Lost Women of Troy
The Labour of Life
Walkers in the Dark
Requiem

OBERON BOOKS
LONDON

WWW.OBERONBOOKS.COM

First published in 2020 by Oberon Books Ltd
521 Caledonian Road, London N7 9RH
Tel: +44 (0) 20 7607 3637 / Fax: +44 (0) 20 7607 3629
e-mail: info@oberonbooks.com
www.oberonbooks.com

A catalogue record for this book is available from the British Library.

PB ISBN: 9781786829146
E ISBN: 9781786829160

Cover design by James Illman
Cover photo by Gadi Dagon

Printed and bound in the UK.

Visit www.oberonbooks.com to read more about all our books and to buy them. You will also find features, author interviews and news of any author events, and you can sign up for e-newsletters and be the first to hear about our new releases.

Printed on FSC® accredited paper

10 9 8 7 6 5 4 3 2 1

Contents

Hanoch Levin: A Short Biographical Note   vii

Suitcase Packers   1

The Lost Women of Troy   73

The Labour of Life   123

Walkers in the Dark   175

Requiem   241

To David Lan, for believing

Thanks

Howard Gooding, Amir Nizar Zuabi, Noam Semel,
Mulli Melzer, George Spender, Dani Tracz, Gal Canetti,
Shimrit Ron and The Hanoch Levin Institute of Israeli Drama

Hanoch Levin:
A Short Biographical Note

By almost unanimous consent, Hanoch Levin is Israel's greatest playwright ever, and he remains, to this day, one of Hebrew culture's most important and diverse artists. His oeuvre encompasses some twenty published volumes, and includes a strikingly wide-ranging variety of genres: comedies and tragedies, satirical cabarets, short stories and other prose, songs, poetry, humorous sketches, radio plays and screenplays. Throughout this comprehensive body of work, Levin created a world full of unmistakable characteristics and formulated a language that is unparalleled in Modern Hebrew.

Levin was born in Tel Aviv, in 1943, the second son to parents who fled Poland in the 1930s. The impoverished family lived in a small apartment in the south of the city. His father, a religious Jew, owned a grocery store and struggled to provide for the family. When he died suddenly, Hanoch, who was only thirteen, went to work to help support the family, and continued his studies at evening school. He abandoned the religious lifestyle completely at a young age, and after his compulsory military service he went to Tel Aviv University. In 1965, he began publishing poetry in literary journals, and wrote satirical features for the student newspaper. This was the beginning of a prolific writing career that would continue right up to his death.

The Six-Day War, in June of 1967, which marked a turning point in the evolution of the State of Israel, was to be a landmark event in Levin's own life. Shortly after the war, at the age of 24, he wrote the political cabaret *You, Me and the Next War*, which sharply scorned Israel's euphoric reaction to its victory in the war, and shattered the ethos of heroism and patriotic sacrifice. Levin was one of the first Israeli voices to criticize Israel's occupation of the Palestinian territories and its dire consequences for both sides. As a result of the cabaret, as well as two others that followed, Levin began to gain a reputation as a talented but controversial artist.

Alongside the cabarets Levin began writing plays, mostly comedies at first, such as *Ya'acoby and Leidental*, *A Winter Funeral*, and *Suitcase Packers*–comedies, but invariably tinged with biting criticism of Israeli society. In the early 1970s, Levin also began directing his plays, mostly meeting enthusiastic audience and acquiring critical acclaim. It was during these years that he developed his distinct theatrical language, as both playwright and director, and the name Levin began to be associated with unique, high-quality theatre.

Toward the end of the 1970s and early 1980s, Levin staged his plays *Execution*, *The Torments of Job* and *The Great Whore of Babylon*, which portrayed ruthless, cruel, and often bloody scenes, although even these were not devoid of a macabre humour. While audience members were frequently shocked, Levin's unique blend of horror and humour, colloquial language and poetic eloquence, positioned him as a one-of-a-kind dramatist. These were the first of Levin's great plays–tragedies, human dramas, mythologies–that engaged with universal themes far beyond the scope of Israeli or Jewish reality. He went on to write and direct incessantly, working on both dramas and comedies–and a constant mingling of dramatic genres. His status as a leading playwright in Israel (and director of his own plays) became firmly established, in particular after his productions of *The Child Dreams*, *Walkers in the Dark*, and *Requiem*. In the last few years of his life, there was no longer any question that this was an extraordinary phenomenon in the Israeli cultural landscape.

In 1997, when Levin was diagnosed with cancer, an initiative to publish his complete works was launched, and almost thirty previously unknown plays were discovered in his files. All the same, the 16-volume edition was completed and published in 1999, shortly before his death. Levin continued writing right up to his final days, and even began directing his play *The Lamenters* from his hospital bed, but he died before he could complete his work.

Since his death in 1999, more and more of his plays continue to appear on Israeli stages, alongside new productions of his classics, and his work has also reached audiences worldwide. Plays by Levin have been translated into over 20 languages, there have been hundreds of productions, and every year brings new translations of his works into various languages. International audiences are becoming familiar with Hanoch Levin's world, and he is on his way to joining the ranks of the finest international playwrights.

Hanoch Levin was married three times, and is survived by four children.

Mulli Melzer
Translated by Jessica Cohen

SUITCASE PACKERS

A comedy with eight funerals

Translated from the Hebrew by Naaman Tammuz

This 'comedy with eight funerals,' as Levin defined it, is about
the frustrated hopes, jeopardized plans, disappointed loves of a
group of neighbours living in a district of Tel Aviv. Each of the
characters' stories ends with a far-from-glorious death; those
who stay behind, attending one funeral after another, go on
schlepping their petty lives, waiting their turn.

Cast of Characters

SHABTAI SCHUSTER
BIANCA, *his wife*
NINA, *their daughter*
BELLA, *their daughter*
HENIA GELERNTER
ELHANAN, *her son*
TZVI, *her deceased husband*
MUNYA GLOBCHIK
LOLA, *his wife*
ZIGGY, *their son*
BOBEH, *Munya's mother*
BRUNO HOFSTADTER
TZILA, *his wife*
AMATSIA, *their son*
MOTKE TZHORI
TZIPORA, *his wife*
AVNER TZHORI, *his brother, a hunchback*
ANGELA HOPKINS, *a young American tourist*
ALBERTO PINKUS
ELISHA HOOKER
ALPHONSE HUZLI
A PROSTITUTE
A GRAVEDIGGER
A SECOND GRAVEDIGGER
A STREET SWEEPER
A CLERK
TWO PARAMEDICS
TWO HASIDIC JEWS

Premiere	The Cameri Theatre, Tel Aviv, 1983
Director	Michael Alfreds
Costume and Stage Design	Ruth Dar
Lighting Design	Brian Harris
Music Composition	Rafi Kadishzon

Cast:

SHABTAI / BRUNO	Avraham Plata
BIANCA	Ruth Segal
NINA	Hani Nachmias
BELLA	Tiki Dayan
HENIA	Zaharira Harifai
ELHANAN	Shabtai Conorti
TZVI	Tzvi Pearl
MUNYA	Ilan Dar
LOLA	Shifra Milshtein
ZIGGY	Dov Reizer
BOBEH	Shulamit Adar
TZILA	Ruth Geller
AMATSIA, ALPHONSE	Yehuda Mor
MOTKE	Yossef Carmon
TZIPORA	Hanna rot
AVNER	Aharon Almog
ANGELA	Lesha Rosenberg
ALBERTO	Albert Cohen
ELISHA,	
STREET SWEEPER	Dror Teplitski
PROSTITUTE	Aliza Rosen
HASSIDIC JEW,	
PARAMEDIC,	
GRAVEDIGGER, CLERK	Perri Maroz
HASSIDIC JEW,	
GRAVEDIGGER	Shmuel Edelman
HASSIDIC JEW,	
PARAMEDIC	Tamir Rozanis

Act One

The SCHUSTER household, SHABTAI SCHUSTER is walking slowly in his pyjamas with a newspaper in his hand, followed by his wife BIANCA and BELLA and NINA, his daughters.

BELLA: Dad is ill, he's going to the loo. Four days he's gone without a pooh, maybe he'll finally do one soon.

SHABTAI: I'm heavy.

BIANCA: He's heavy, so heavy.

SHABTAI: Everyone's cheated me.

BIANCA: You have a wife and two daughters, Shabtai.

SHABTAI: Cheated, I tell you. I'm heavy and cheated.

(Kneels down, BIANCA rushes to lift him up, he waves her away.)

BELLA: Dad's praying.

SHABTAI: Lord.

(Pause.)

To be successful.

(Pause.)

Amen.

(Gets up, turns to his wife and daughters. BIANCA walks over and gives him a kiss.)

BIANCA: My man.

(BELLA walks over and gives him a kiss.)

BELLA: Courage.

(NINA wraps her hands around his neck.)

NINA: Joie de vivre.

(Hangs onto him.)

BELLA: Dad's heavy, Nina.

(NINA lets go of him. SHABTAI waves farewell with the hand holding the newspaper.)

SHABTAI: In my youth I used to go. Oh, I went and went. Goodbye everyone. Youth, youth.

(Starts leaving very slowly.)

BIANCA: In his youth he used to go, let me tell you. You two were still little, but he used to go.

(SHABTAI moves further away.)

Oh Shabtai.

BELLA: We believe it, Daddy. We were little, but we believe it.

(SHABTAI exits. ZIGGY's voice from outside.)

ZIGGY: Nina! Ready?

NINA: Going out with Ziggy.

BIANCA: Aren't you going to wait for Dad to come out?

NINA: We made plans.

BELLA: To the cinema, eh? The cinema!

NINA: To see a sad film, I'm not going to laugh tonight.

BIANCA: Not late.

(NINA leaves. BELLA cries.)

Not now, Bella.

(BELLA carries on crying.)

BIANCA: Dad will be out any minute, does he need to see you crying?

BELLA: I want, Mummy. I want.

BIANCA: *(Wipes her face.)*

Your day will come.

BELLA: I want, I want.

BIANCA: You'll get. You'll get.

(SHABTAI enters, newspaper in hand, shuffling along slowly, stops in front of BIANCA and BELLA. BIANCA gives him an inquisitive look.)

SHABTAI: Nothing.

BIANCA: Not even…?

SHABTAI: Not even. Bad for the heart, bad for the heart.

BIANCA: Did you get some enjoyment from the newspaper?

(SHABTAI lets the newspaper fall from his hands, continues walking away slowly, exits.)

BELLA: Dad's stopped reading the newspaper, he's only focused on one thing now.

BIANCA: How he used to read the newspaper and analyse the politics for me. For hours. You don't remember, but I can testify to it.

(SHABTAI enters, takes the newspaper from her hand, continues walking towards the toilet.)

BIANCA: Is there?

SHABTAI: Can't promise.

(Exits.)

BIANCA: My man, I'll testify!

(To BELLA.)

Look at Dad, he's trying and trying and trying, he's not giving up.

(BELLA cries.)

Oh, you silly girl. He'll go and you'll get, you'll see.

Act Two

The kitchen in the GELERNTER household. ELHANAN, a large fat young man, enters in his pyjamas and drinks some water. His mother HENIA enters.

HENIA: Elhanan, what are you doing up at night drinking like a horse?

ELHANAN: I had a bad dream.

HENIA: Don't dream, get married.

(Exits.)

ELHANAN: *(To himself.)*

Well I dream about a wife every single night. A grey dream, but very passionate. Lots of passion. And that makes me thirsty.

(Drinks.)

Now I'm bloated.

(HENIA enters.)

HENIA: I want to throw up. I'm worried about my heart.

ELHANAN: The heart was created to serve us.

HENIA: Not in my case.

(Exits. NINA and ZIGGY enter in the street opposite, stop by the door to NINA's house, kiss.)

NINA: Dad hasn't gone for four days.

ZIGGY: Grandma's got pneumonia.

NINA: Good night.

(ZIGGY grabs her breast.)

ZIGGY: I'm waiting for an answer. Tell your father that the i…i…i…income will be fine.

(NINA exits. ZIGGY leaves in the other direction. ELHANAN drinks.)

ELHANAN: To Switzerland!

(Eats bread and sausage. HENIA enters.)

HENIA: You're young, you've got an appetite. I'm just nauseous.

ELHANAN: What did you use to eat at weddings then, old woman?

HENIA: Who ate anything? Who slept? Who's ever enjoyed themselves!

(Exits. ELHANAN eats.)

ELHANAN: To Switzerland!

(Exits. HENIA enters.)

HENIA: Can't throw up. Good times. What am I even asking for? To go dancing? To buy a villa? I'm just asking to throw up.

(Eats bread.)

There. So there's something to throw up. Lots.

(ELHANAN enters fully dressed, carrying a suitcase.)

Where to?

ELHANAN: Switzerland.

HENIA: At night?

ELHANAN: They're waiting for me.

HENIA: Youngsters, eh? The blood's flowing nicely, eh? Leaving me all alone.

ELHANAN: I'll write.

HENIA: You won't write.

ELHANAN: I will write.

HENIA: Enough.

(Turns to leave.)

ELHANAN: What about a farewell?

(HENIA stops, ELHANAN hugs her.)

HENIA: Squeeze tight, good, so that I throw up.

(ELHANAN loosens his grip. Turns to leave.)

Yes yes, and I'll die here in the meantime.

ELHANAN: I might die too.

HENIA: You won't die, you're built like a tank.

(Exits, ELHANAN leaves in the opposite direction.)

Act Three

Night. A bus stop. ELHANAN enters with a suitcase. AMATSIA shows up in front of him, also carrying a suitcase.

AMATSIA: Hello, Elhanan.

ELHANAN: Amatsia?

AMATSIA: Yes.

ELHANAN: Aren't you in America?

AMATSIA: I came for a visit. My parents are old and I want to introduce them to my American fiancé.

ELHANAN: Where is she?

AMATSIA: She's coming in a week. And you?

ELHANAN: Me?

AMATSIA: Where to, I mean?

ELHANAN: Just out, getting some air.

AMATSIA: Abroad?

ELHANAN: Why not. What do you think about Switzerland?

AMATSIA: What can I say about Switzerland? Weren't you going to get married at some point? To a student?

ELHANAN: She went to Switzerland.

(AMATSIA faints.)

Amatsia! Amatsia!

(AMATSIA comes to.)

AMATSIA: Forgive me. I'm exhausted from the trip. Maybe I'm excited. And maybe I'm sick.

(A PROSTITUTE enters, stands at a distance, looking at them.)

ELHANAN: You're pale.

(The PROSTITUTE comes closer.)

PROSTITUTE: Both of you for a hundred and fifty.

(AMATSIA picks up his suitcase.)

AMATSIA: I'm going. My old parents are waiting for me at home.

ELHANAN: Send them my regards.

AMATSIA: Goodbye, Elhanan. So long. Enjoy yourself.

ELHANAN: Enjoy your holiday.

(AMATSIA leaves. The PROSTITUTE approaches ELHANAN.)

PROSTITUTE: Hey honey.

ELHANAN: I'm on my way to Switzerland.

PROSTITUTE: Some people are like that.

(Shows him a breast.)

ELHANAN: And I need to preserve my freshness.

(The PROSTITUTE lifts her skirt.)

ELHANAN: I have a long trip ahead of me.

(The PROSTITUTE shakes her hips. He gets down on his knees in front of her.)

And I wouldn't want to leave all my strength behind with you.

(Touches her thigh.)

Filthy flesh.

(The PROSTITUTE slaps his cheek.)

Whore.

PROSTITUTE: Come! Switzerland! Eat me out! One hundred!

(Pause. She leaves. ELHANAN follows her.)

Act Four

Dawn at the bus stop. TWO HASIDIC JEWS who have recently woken up rush – anxiously – to the synagogue while mumbling.

HASIDIC JEWS: I give thanks before You, King living and eternal, for You have returned within me my soul with compassion; abundant is Your faithfulness!

(Old BOBEH GLOBCHIK enters, dressed in a night gown with a coat on top, and holding a small suitcase. Behind her walk her son MUNYA, his wife LOLA and their son ZIGGY.)

LOLA: Grandma's going to a sanatorium for lung patients. She'll breath fresh air, get better and come back safe and sound.

(BOBEH stops. Pause. Turns back. Starts retracing her steps. MUNYA blocks her path.)

MUNYA: No, Mum, that way.

(BOBEH stops for a moment, tries to turn back again. MUNYA blocks her path.)

No, Mum, that way, there.

LOLA: Grandma will get better and come back.

ZIGGY: G…g…g…grandma…

MUNYA: What's that?

LOLA: He's not saying anything. I hope it's clear that we're sending her away because of you, Ziggy. We need a spare room in case you get married.

ZIGGY: G…g…

LOLA: We heard you. I'm going up to make breakfast. Come, Ziggy.

(LOLA and ZIGGY exit.)

MUNYA: *(To BOBEH.)*

The most important thing for me is that you're not upset.

(Tickles her under her chin.)

Right?

(Tickles her under her armpit.)

Eh, Mum? Are we laughing a little? New day? Eh? Light? Morning? Going to get better? To rest? Me working like a horse and you resting? With my money? To rest? Eh, Mummy? Are we laughing? Entertained? Is life a joke, Mummy? But a joke that costs money, lots of money, eh?! Lots of money! The bus is coming.

(Escorts her to the bus.)

We'll come and visit on Saturday.

(Kisses her forehead. BOBEH exits. MUNYA watches her go for a moment, then exits as well. Pause. BOBEH comes back in with the suitcase, walking very very slowly back towards the house. MUNYA enters suddenly, blocking her path.)

Escaping, Mum?! Spitting in my face?!

(A STREET SWEEPER passes by with a rubbish cart.)

Into the bin! Hey, sweeper, take this rubbish away!

(The SWEEPER approaches BOBEH with his cart, MUNYA lifts her up, puts her in the cart.)

Here, to the bin!

STREET SWEEPER: Your mother?

(Lifts her up out of the cart.)

All right, we've had a little laugh. No time, rubbish, rubbish.

(Exits with the cart.)

MUNYA: The second bus is coming.

(Escorts her to the bus. Hugs her.)

Mum!

(Crying. Lets go of her.)

All right, the bus is leaving. Goodbye.

(BOBEH walks to the bus. MUNYA waves. Stops. Bursts out crying again.)

Mum, you were the last one separating between me and death. Mummy, mummy.

(LOLA and ZIGGY enter.)

LOLA: The egg's getting cold.

ZIGGY: I don't have an a...a...a...appetite.

LOLA: OK, we heard you. Come on, Munya.

MUNYA: You two can vouch for the fact that a man has to eat.

LOLA: Come on already, you pigs. To stuff yourselves. To stink at Lola's.

MUNYA: My eternal Lola.

LOLA: You'd better believe I'm eternal.

ZIGGY: Nothing c...could be c...c...c...clearer.

(They exit.)

Act Five

Early evening. A GRAVEDIGGER enters, slowly pulling a cart carrying the body of SHABTAI SCHUSTER. Behind the cart walk BIANCA, BELLA, NINA, MUNYA, LOLA, ZIGGY, BRUNO and TZILA HOFSTADTER AMATSIA's parents, AMATSIA, ELHANAN, HENIA, ALBERTO PINKUS, AVNER TZHORI the hunchback, his short fat brother MOTKE TZHORI and his fat wife TZIPORA. The funeral procession stops in front of the SCHUSTER residence. PINKUS stands in front of everyone, ready to eulogize.

LOLA: *(To MUNYA, whispering.)*

They say that to his dying day he never managed to go.

(To TZILA, whispering.)

He never managed to go even to his dying day, that's what they say.

TZILA: *(To TZIPORA, whispering.)*

How many days was that in total?

TZILA: *(To LOLA, whispering.)*

He never managed to go, to his dying day.

TZIPORA: *(Whispering.)*

How many days was that in total?

LOLA: *(To TZILA and TZIPORA, whispering.)*

Over a week.

ALBERTO: *(Addressing the crowd.)*

Dear Shabtai Schuster. Today we bid you farewell.

(Long pause.)

MUNYA: Carry on.

BIANCA: Why has he stopped?

ALBERTO: I'm done.

GRAVEDIGGER: *(Sings.)*

Righteousness shall go before Him...

(Pulls the cart and exits. Everyone apart from AVNER TZHORI exits after him. He stands, watching them leave. BELLA enters in a rush.)

BELLA: I told you to stop following me.

AVNER: I came for the funeral.

BELLA: Ptui!

(Exits.)

AVNER: *(To himself.)*

A little excess of flesh on my back has ruined my life. It's not a deficit which has darkened the skies of my fate, but a surplus.

(MOTKE enters.)

MOTKE: What's up?

AVNER: Going back home.

MOTKE: What's eating you? Why aren't you calm?

AVNER: I'm calm and pale.

MOTKE: Careful, Avner, don't mess around with your paleness.

(TZIPORA enters. She's pregnant.)

TZIPORA: What's going on? We're missing the funeral.

MOTKE: Messing around with his paleness.

TZIPORA: God doesn't know who to give health to.

AVNER: I'm not healthy.

TZIPORA: We heard you. Forty years old – and alive.

MOTKE: Be calm and act accordingly. You're my brother, look at me and calm down.

AVNER: Can I speak to you in private?

MOTKE: My wife is me, I am my wife.

AVNER: All right.

(Pause.)

I'll find myself a room and go and live alone.

MOTKE: Any time you like.

AVNER: Because soon you're also due to have…

MOTKE: Any time you like.

AVNER: That's all.

TZIPORA: The funeral, Motke.

(MOTKE and TZIPORA turn to go. MOTKE stops and turns to AVNER.)

MOTKE: Look at me and calm down.

(Exits with his arm around TZIPORA. From the other side enters a PROSTITUTE, looks on from a distance.)

PROSTITUTE: Did someone die?

AVNER: A neighbour.

PROSTITUTE: A worm will be sucking him off tonight, may he rest in peace. What about you?

AVNER: *(Takes out a bank note from his wallet, shuts his eyes.)*

Forgive me. Forgive me. Forgive me.

(Walks after the PROSTITUTE. They both exit.)

Act Six

The HOFSTADTER household. Night. AMATSIA enters in his pyjamas, followed by BRUNO.

BRUNO: Where is she, Amatsia? A week has passed, two weeks have passed.

AMATSIA: She should be arriving any day.

BRUNO: Why bother standing by the window? She'll send a telegram when she arrives.

AMATSIA: I'm getting some air.

BRUNO: *(Puts a hand on his shoulder.)*

You need to go in for some checks, Amatsia.

AMATSIA: If the dizziness doesn't go away by the end of the week, I'll go in for some checks.

BRUNO: Your mother and I saved up a bit. We've decided to give you two a flat.

AMATSIA: She has one of her own. We're going to live in America. I told you I've only come for a visit.

BRUNO: I thought you'd have a change of heart.

AMATSIA: It's small here, Dad. In America I'm going to start a business.

BRUNO: What business?

AMATSIA: I don't know yet. I want to stand at the window by myself for a bit, Dad.

BRUNO: Good night.

(Exits. ELHANAN passes by in the street, sees AMATSIA at the window, stops in front of him.)

ELHANAN: Sick, or ready for bed?

AMATSIA: Sick, if I'm not mistaken.

ELHANAN: The dizziness?

AMATSIA: Just when I'm visiting.

ELHANAN: And the American?

AMATSIA: She got held up a bit.

(Pause.)

ELHANAN: Tell me, Amatsia, is she pretty?

AMATSIA: Yes.

ELHANAN: Blonde?

AMATSIA: Yes.

ELHANAN: Maybe she's also well off?

AMATSIA: Yes.

(Pause.)

ELHANAN: Tell me, should I go to Switzerland?

AMATSIA: Why not.

ELHANAN: It's pretty there, isn't it?

AMATSIA: Yes.

ELHANAN: But apart from it being pretty, should I?

AMATSIA: Do you mean, to live there?

ELHANAN: Maybe.

AMATSIA: Your student went there, didn't she? You can ask her.

ELHANAN: Should I go to see her?

AMATSIA: Why not?

ELHANAN: What for?

AMATSIA: I don't know.

ELHANAN: Me neither. Thinking about women's always been my hobby. It's something that's easy to do and not as dangerous as actually dealing with real women.

AMATSIA: But if you love her...

ELHANAN: I do love her. But I need to come to her feeling fresh. And for that I need to freshen up. But freshen up from what? I haven't exerted myself, I haven't sweated, I haven't tired myself, but nevertheless I feel that I'm not fresh, not fresh.

(Pause.)

Listen, I'm telling you...I'm telling you...

(Pause.)

Good night, and good health.

AMATSIA: Good night.

(ELHANAN exits. AMATSIA remains standing at the window, and he sings a sad American song quietly to himself. BRUNO enters in his pyjamas.)

BRUNO: Come to sleep, Amatsia.

AMATSIA: You don't need to worry, Dad.

BRUNO: What do we have to be worried about.

AMATSIA: Exactly. Don't be. I want to stand by the window for a bit.

BRUNO: We're going to sleep, good night.

AMATSIA: Good night.

(BRUNO turns to go, stops.)

BRUNO: You're our hope. You.

(Exits. AMATSIA remains standing at the window, quietly singing a sad American song. Music can be heard from the other room. BRUNO in pyjamas and TZILA in a night gown enter in each other's arms dancing slowly to the music. They talk as they dance.)

TZILA: Amatsia, my dear son, tonight's thirty years since Dad and I got married.

BRUNO: Thirty years ago there was a ceremony...

TZILA: A man and a woman got married...

BRUNO: A year later they had a son...

TZILA: They gave him all their love...

BRUNO: The child grew up...

TZILA: They grew old...

BRUNO: And the child remained their only hope...

TZILA: Their only hope.

AMATSIA: My dear parents, wait until she comes...

(Hugs them, joins in the dance.)

TZILA: And when she comes...

BRUNO: And when she comes...

AMATSIA: There will be a ceremony...

TZILA: A man and a woman will get married...

(The three of them dance out.)

Act Seven

Night-time in a night club. NINA is dancing with ELISHA HOOKER, a young man.

NINA: You're light.

ELISHA: I like dancing, and I also like a good book.

(ZIGGY enters, sits on the side, eating peanuts and watching them.)

ELISHA: So what do you, like, do?

NINA: Nothing. I read, I mold.

ELISHA: What do you mold?

NINA: Molding. Ceramics.

ELISHA: Ah.

NINA: I'm not in a hurry, not rushing like everyone, what's so urgent? What's all this chasing? Don't you think?

ELISHA: Sure.

NINA: What do you do?

ELISHA: Read a bit, write a bit.

NINA: Poems?

ELISHA: To myself, at night.

NINA: And in the morning?

ELISHA: Doctor.

NINA: You say 'doctor' so dismissively. You're really different.

ELISHA: Because who are doctors anyway? It's all a myth.

NINA: You're so different.

(They carry on dancing. The music stops. NINA and ELISHA go back to their seats. NINA sees ZIGGY.)

NINA: Hello, Ziggy.

ZIGGY: Hello.

NINA: This is Elisha.

ZIGGY: Ziggy.

NINA: You alone?

ZIGGY: Huh? Yes.

ELISHA: We should go. I have an operation in the morning.

NINA: Of course. See you, Ziggy.

ZIGGY: See you.

(NINA and ELISHA exit. The music comes back on. ZIGGY sits a moment longer, gets up, exits as well, stands at the entrance to the club, watches NINA and ELISHA leaving. BOBEH enters slowly, wearing a night gown and above it a coat, carrying a small suitcase in her hand. ZIGGY is stunned.)

ZIGGY: G...g...g...grandma.

BOBEH: *(Stops, looks at him.)*

Zigginiu

(ZIGGY hugs her, takes the suitcase from her.)

ZIGGY: You ran away from the sanatorium, g...g...g... grandma.

(Stands hugging her for a moment. The music keeps playing. For a moment they look like they're dancing motionlessly. ZIGGY exits with BOBEH. From the other side enter BIANCA SCHUSTER and

26

ALBERTO PINKUS. ALBERTO is supporting her elbow. They stop at the entrance to the club.)

ALBERTO: Shall we go in?

BIANCA: Don't pressure me, Pinkus, I still can't fully bear to see people dancing.

ALBERTO: I respect your feelings.

BIANCA: We ate dinner together in a restaurant, even that was already too much for me.

ALBERTO: Eating isn't too much, Mrs Schuster.

BIANCA: Why don't you call me Bianca?

ALBERTO: I'll call you Bianca if you call me Alberto.

BIANCA: Alberto.

ALBERTO: Bianca Pepperonca.

BIANCA: Bianca Pepperonca, that's what he used to call me, the deceased.

ALBERTO: Sorry, I don't want to hurt your feelings.

BIANCA: Why not, go ahead.

ALBERTO: Maybe I'll take Bianca Cucumberonca

BIANCA: We're sticking with vegetables.

ALBERTO: If you don't mind.

BIANCA: Thank you, Alberto. You're a considerate man.

ALBERTO: I'll walk you home.

BIANCA: You're not angry?

ALBERTO: I understand your feelings.

(BIANCA strokes his cheek. They exit.)

Act Eight

Dawn. Bus stop. BOBEH walks in slowly, dressed in a night gown with a coat above it and a small suitcase in her hand. Behind her walk MUNYA, LOLA and ZIGGY.

MUNYA: This time you're staying there, Mum, eating well, breathing fresh air until you get better, right?

LOLA: You don't need to come here, Mum, we'll come to you.

MUNYA: On Saturday, if it's a nice day.

LOLA: I'm going to make breakfast. Come on, Ziggy.

(Hugs BOBEH, ZIGGY kisses BOBEH. LOLA and ZIGGY exit.)

MUNYA: Don't give us so much trouble again, Mum, you can see how hard it is for Lola, working like a horse, running around, tidying, and you with your games. One more time, Mum – and you're going to the closed ward. The bus is here.

(Hugs and kisses her. BOBEH exits. MUNYA waves goodbye to her. From the other side enters AVNER TZHORI with a large suitcase. MUNYA turns to leave, sees him.)

Hello, Tzhori.

AVNER: Hello, Mr Globchik.

MUNYA: Travelling? A holiday?

AVNER: Moving flat.

MUNYA: Where to?

AVNER: Not far.

MUNYA: With Motke and Tzipora?

AVNER: Alone.

MUNYA: Well, then good luck.

AVNER: To you too.

MUNYA: Thanks, I'm already lucky.

(MUNYA exits. AVNER walks to the bus stop. BOBEH enters from the other side, walks past him, they look at each other for a moment, AVNER stops at the bus stop, BOBEH carries on walking. MUNYA enters and stands in her way.)

All right, Mum. Tomorrow morning – to the closed ward.

(Exits with BOBEH. AVNER sits at the bus stop. Morning arrives. A STREET SWEEPER passes by. A CLERK goes to work. Noon. Afternoon. The CLERK returns from work. Early evening. The light diminishes. AVNER TZHORI keeps sitting. Evening. The PROSTITUTE passes by, lingers next to AVNER. He doesn't notice her. The PROSTITUTE leaves. Night. BELLA enters, sees AVNER, turns to leave, has a change of heart, stops, approaches him. AVNER stands up.)

BELLA: I'm sorry if I hurt you. I didn't mean to offend anyone.

(Pause.)

I just wanted you to know, it's not going to work out. You mustn't hope.

(Pause.)

You understand that you mustn't hope, right?

AVNER: How do I do that?

BELLA: I don't know, I understand you, but I don't know what advice to give you.

AVNER: What will you do if I dream about you anyway?

BELLA: If you dream about me?

(Cries.)

AVNER: Forgive me. I didn't mean to offend anyone.

(Pause.)

Does it offend you if I dream about you?

(Pause.)

I promise not to dream about you anymore.

(Takes a step towards her.)

Really, I promise…

BELLA: Don't come near me.

(Stops crying.)

Sorry, I didn't mean to offend anyone.

AVNER: No problem.

BELLA: But you really are stupid. If you're going to be dreaming, you might as well dream about the very best.

AVNER: You are the very best.

(BELLA laughs.)

There. Laughing so warmly. I swear you're the very best.

BELLA: Have you ever been to the cinema?

AVNER: Ah, those from the cinema. There are things I don't even dare to dream about.

BELLA: That means I'm the pinnacle of your dreams.

AVNER: Absolutely.

BELLA: *(Crying.)*

The pinnacle of his dreams.

AVNER: I won't dream about you any more, Bella.

(BELLA exits.)

I promise, I won't…

(Pause. Picks up his suitcase. Hesitates for a moment. Exits.)

Act Nine

The GELERNTER household. Night. HENIA GELERNTER enters in a night gown. She's pale and looks terrible.

HENIA: *(Mumbling to herself.)* On my tombstone just write: 'Died at age eight'! I never lived after the age of eight! Write 'Died at age eight'!

(TZVI, her dead husband, enters. A young man about thirty years old, dressed like a tourist. HENIA sees him and stops in amazement.)

HENIA: Tzvi?

TZVI: Yes

(HENIA almost runs into his arms but stops herself. TZVI reaches his hands out to her.)

Come, Henia.

HENIA: Tzvi…Tzvi…

(At a loss, brushes her hand through her hair, on her face, on the night gown.)

Tzvi…I'm so embarrassed.

TZVI: Aren't you my wife?

HENIA: I am your wife, Tzvi, I am your wife, and I've been faithful to you all these years you haven't been with me… it's just that you haven't changed since then and I…

(Gestures with her hands in yearning and despair.)

I should have died with you.

TZVI: Who would have looked after Elhanan?

HENIA: Elhanan worries me. He's not getting married, he doesn't have a flat.

TZVI: Come, Henia. Let's go for a walk and you can tell me everything. I want to treat you to some American soft-serve ice cream.

HENIA: Oh, Tzvi, you've found the wrong person to eat ice cream with. The heart, Tzvi, the heart, the sugar, the blood pressure. Are you healthy?

TZVI: Yes, thank god. All the dead are healthy.

HENIA: Ah, I envy you.

TZVI: Come, Henia, come for a little walk with me.

(Holds his hands out to her. HENIA takes one step towards him.)

HENIA: Tzvi. My husband. You're so handsome. Darkness is slowly descending around me, Tzvi, you've been my only light from inside all this time.

(Takes another step towards him.)

You're so handsome.

(Stands on her tiptoes, holds her arms out to her sides.)

Tzvi, all the yearning…all the memories…you're awakening it all in me again, my love…the world used to be…the senses used to be sharp…all the colours, all the freshness…

TZVI: Come, Henia…

HENIA: And now look what's happened to me, Tzvi…

(Bursts into tears.)

I'm so embarrassed…I'm so embarrassed …I'm so embarrassed…

TZVI: Just for a walk, Henia. Ice cream, a bit of gossip. No touching, just a walk.

HENIA: You're like my son...

TZVI: In the sky it's Saturday and the evening is approaching...

(Starts moving further away, his voice weakening.)

Come with me to eat American soft-serve ice cream...

HENIA: *(Stops crying.)*

Save me a portion, Tzvi!

(TZVI exits.)

Tzvi!

(ELHANAN enters in his pyjamas.)

ELHANAN: Mum!

(HENIA turns to him.)

HENIA: I dreamt about Dad. He wanted me to go for a walk with him.

(Her face hardens again.)

Yes, yes, they're going to take your mother away, Elhanan. Instead of looking after her health, you're opening and closing suitcases! Watch out, Elhanan!

(Turns to leave, stops.)

And don't write: 'At a ripe old age!' No 'old' and no 'ripe'! 'Died at age eight' – and that's that!

(Exits. In the street under their window AMATSIA enters, wearing pyjamas, with a robe over them, supported on either side by BRUNO

and TZILA. His head is spinning, it's hard for him to stand. While walking he sees ELHANAN in the window.)

AMATSIA: Hello, Elhanan. I'm going to hospital.

TZILA: Elhanan, if an American girl shows up and asks about Amatsia, we'll be right back.

(AMATSIA laughs a short quiet laugh to himself.)

ELHANAN: Perhaps you need some help?

BRUNO: We're taking a taxi, thank you.

TZILA: Just tell her please that we'll be right back.

(AMATSIA collapses in BRUNO's arms. BRUNO starts crying, regains his composure.)

BRUNO: We'll be right back.

(Exits with AMATSIA and TZILA.)

Act Ten

Street. Dawn. Old BOBEH enters wearing a night gown and above it a coat, with a small suitcase in her hand. Next to her is MUNYA, holding her arm. LOLA is on her balcony.

MUNYA: And now, Mum, to the closed ward, and this time I'm taking you all the way there, they'll lock you in and you won't ever be able to get out again.

(BOBEH stops, refuses to keep walking. MUNYA pulls her, she resists. He lifts her up.)

This time we'll put an end to it…once and for all…

(Exits with her. The sun rises, morning. TZILA and BRUNO enter, TZILA leaning on his shoulder and crying.)

LOLA: What happened, Mrs Hofstadter?

BRUNO: Amatsia's going to have an operation to remove a brain tumour.

LOLA: Oh, when will you have some peace and quiet, when will you have some peace and quiet.

TZILA: *(Crying.)*

And when will you, Mrs Globchik?

(BRUNO and TZILA exit. MUNYA enters the street, stops, deep in thought.)

LOLA: That was quick.

(Pause.)

Come, come in, lunch is ready.

(Pause.)

Munya, the food's getting cold.

MUNYA: Is that all you've got to say to me, 'the food's getting cold'? 'The food's getting cold', 'the watermelon's getting warm', 'the bread's on the counter', 'the egg's on the hob'? Is that what you've got to say?

LOLA: The old woman's already turned him against me. Oh, to hell with everything, let me die!

(Exits. AVNER TZHORI enters the street with a suitcase. MUNYA looks at him for a moment and leaves in the direction of his house. TZIPORA enters behind AVNER.)

TZIPORA: No, it's not going to work like that. You take all your things in one go and say goodbye, you don't take them one suitcase at a time every couple of days.

AVNER: I don't have enough to pay movers, and I myself don't have the strength. In a week I'll be done with everything.

TZIPORA: You have no intention of leaving, that's the whole issue.

AVNER: You can see I'm leaving.

TZIPORA: I can't see anything! A normal person takes all their things and says goodbye.

(MOTKE enters.)

MOTKE: What's all the shouting?

TZIPORA: Your brother, your brother, your brother! This will all end with me having a miscarriage! And that'll be the end of the Tzhori dynasty! No one to continue the Tzhori dynasty! All done!

MOTKE: Why don't you calm down, Avner?! It's about time! The devil take you, baby murderer, when will you be calm, when?!

(LOLA comes out onto her balcony screaming.)

LOLA: In the middle of the soup! In the middle of the soup! In the middle of the soup! In the middle of the soup!

(ZIGGY enters, tries to quiet her down.)

ZIGGY: A...a...a...a...a...

LOLA: *(Carries on screaming.)*

In the middle of the soup! In the middle of the soup!

(ZIGGY takes her outside. People start coming out into the street. AVNER, MOTKE and TZIPORA, who are already in the street, are joined by BRUNO, TZILA, BIANCA, NINA, BELLA, HENIA and ELHANAN.)

BELLA: Who? Who?

HENIA: Munya Globchik

(The GRAVEDIGGER enters, pulling a cart carrying MUNYA's body covered with a sheet. Behind the cart walks LOLA, crying, propped up by ZIGGY. Behind them is ALBERTO PINKUS. All the rest join the funeral procession. The procession stops opposite MUNYA's house.)

LOLA: *(Crying, quietly.)*

Munya...Munya...Munya...

(ALBERTO stands in front of everyone, ready to eulogize.)

TZIPORA: You hand in two watches to be repaired, eighty lira.

BIANCA: One person hands in two watches to be repaired, another person dies.

HENIA: At least he lived a little, played cards. And me?

ALBERTO: Dear Munya Globchik. Today we bid you farewell.

(Pause.)

MOTKE: *(Shouts.)*

Replace the eulogizer!

ALBERTO: Stop shouting you thug!

MOTKE: A man isn't a bug!

GRAVEDIGGER: Righteousness shall go before Him...

(Pulls the cart and exits. Everyone exits apart from AVNER who remains standing next to his suitcase. From the opposite side enters old BOBEH, suitcase in hand. She walks past AVNER, stops, chuckles at him, puts down her suitcase, stretches, picks up her suitcase and exits. AVNER also picks up his suitcase and exits.)

Act Eleven

Dawn. In the street, next to the bus stop. NINA and BELLA enter, NINA dressed for a trip, a purse in her hand, followed by ELISHA HOOKER and ZIGGY, each carrying a suitcase. They stand by the bus stop.

ELISHA: We'll take a taxi to the airport.

BELLA: In Rome it's Spring.

NINA: We'll only be in Rome for a week. Elisha has other commitments in Vienna.

(To ZIGGY.)

You can put the suitcase down, Ziggy, thanks for your help.

(Takes him aside.)

Ziggy, you know how I feel about you. I want you to know that nothing about my feelings towards you has changed.

ZIGGY: H...h...how can that be?

NINA: That's how it is. You've always been a friend and that's what you'll always be.

BELLA: You need to get going, Nina.

NINA: Yes. Look after my sister, Ziggy.

BELLA: *(Rudely.)*

Thanks a lot for your concern, Ninushka.

(Approaches her, they speak quietly.)

God will pay you back for everything. God isn't going to forget my sleepless nights.

NINA: Take pills, Bella. Take a whole jar of pills and go to sleep.

BELLA: One day you go to Europe with a smile on your face, one day you come back to Asia with tears in your eyes, it's okay.

NINA: I'm not sure you'll have the pleasure.

BELLA: God will help me and I'll have the pleasure. God remembers everything.

NINA: God-God-God, blah-blah-blah.

BELLA: *(Cries.)*

My turn to laugh has got to come at some point, it's got to…

NINA: Got to? Says who? I've got to eat tasty quiches in Vienna with my doctor husband, that's what's got to happen.

(Loudly.)

There there, Bella, don't cry. The farewell's difficult for you, but we'll see each other again soon.

BELLA: *(Carries on crying.)*

Oh, Ninushka, Ninushka, it'll be so empty without you.

ELISHA: Taxi!

(Picks up the two suitcases.)

Goodbye everyone, anatomy degrees in Europe are very good, first and foremost because there are more dissections there.

(Exits. NINA blows a kiss and exits after him. Pause.)

BELLA: Why didn't the two of you get married then?

ZIGGY: I don't know myself. I was sure everything was sorted in terms of the i…i…i…income.

BELLA: Turns out it wasn't.

ZIGGY: T…t…turns out that even if you have an i…i…i… income, there are those with e…even more i…i…income.

BELLA: What will you do with your i…i…income now?

ZIGGY: I don't think I'm going to answer you.

(He exits. BELLA sits at the bus stop. The sun rises. Morning. ALBERTO PINKUS enters with LOLA GLOBCHIK, holding a full basket of groceries in one hand and lightly supporting her elbow with the other.)

ALBERTO: Why, I'll walk you to your house, Mrs Globchik, I have time and it's no trouble for me.

(Sees BELLA.)

Hello, Bella.

(BELLA ignores him contemptuously.)

How's your mother? Feeling all right? Please send her best wishes from Alberto.

(BELLA walks off with blatant contempt. LOLA laughs.)

LOLA: A devil, Mr Pinkus, a devil. Women need to watch out for you.

ALBERTO: *(Laughs with enjoyment.)*

After all I am a child. And please call me Alberto.

LOLA: No no, I'm being careful.

(ALBERTO presses his body to hers. She laughs.)

In any case, we've arrived. Thank you for escorting me, and excuse me for not inviting you upstairs now.

ALBERTO: Of course. I wouldn't want to hurt your feelings.

LOLA: Thank you.

ALBERTO: *(Hands her the basket.)*

So Saturday evening.

LOLA: At eight.

(She exits. AMATSIA enters wearing pyjamas with a coat on top, supported by BRUNO and TZILA. AMATSIA's head is bandaged, his face is grim.)

ALBERTO: Hello, Amatsia. Back from hospital, all better.

(AMATSIA looks at him for a moment with a vacant stare, doesn't recognize him.)

Alberto.

AMATSIA: Ah

(Pause.)

'Dear Amatsia Hofstadter, today we bid you farewell. Dear Amatsia Hofstadter…'

(Stops.)

ALBERTO: *(Tries to laugh along.)*

You rascal, Amatsia.

(BRUNO and TZILA lead AMATSIA out. ALBERTO exits too.)

Act Twelve

Morning, in the street. TZIPORA enters with a pram, stands, rocks it. AVNER enters with a small trolley with a suitcase perched on it. Stops next to TZIPORA.

TZIPORA: Spring's here, and he's still moving out.

AVNER: *(Peers at the baby in the pushchair.)*

Coochy coo.

TZIPORA: You're planting nightmares in my son's soul, just leave.

AVNER: My son would have been born with the soul of an artist. All his father's dreams, all his sensitivity, would have been invested into him.

TZIPORA: An artist's soul – maybe. A hump on his back – definitely.

(Looks back.)

Oh, a funeral. They're planting nightmares in my son's soul. I've got to emigrate from here, I tell you. You lot are either sick or you're dead. Who is it this time? Amatsia Hofstadter, who else. Brain tumour. Yuck!

(To the baby.)

Coochy coo. It's not daddy, it's not daddy, hush hush hush.

(Exits with the pram. The GRAVEDIGGER enters, pulling a cart carrying AMATSIA's body covered with a sheet. Behind the cart walk BRUNO, TZILA who's crying, BIANCA, BELLA, LOLA, ALBERTO PINKUS, ZIGGY, HENIA, ELHANAN and MOTKE. The funeral procession stops at the entrance of the HOFSTADTER residence. ALBERTO stands in front of everyone, ready to eulogize.)

BIANCA: *(Loudly.)*

And I'd happily skip his eulogy this time.

LOLA: Mr Pinkus is a writer and a scholar.

BIANCA: And a crook, that's true!

(Murmuring and hushing sounds from the gathered folk.)

MOTKE: Shh! Respect for the deceased!

BIANCA: A simple crook!

LOLA: Not everyone who doesn't marry someone is a crook.

BIANCA: Not everyone who goes with one person after going with another person is an honest man!

ALBERTO: Dear Amatsia Hofstadter…

(ANGELA enters. A pretty tourist, well-dressed with a small purse and a camera.)

LOLA: The American!

(Everyone turns to look at her. She takes a step towards them.)

ANGELA: *(In an American accent.)*

Excuse me…

LOLA: Obviously!

ANGELA: Is this the old quarter of the city?

LOLA: She arrived just in time for the funeral. You got here in time. Exactly. You haven't missed anything. Come, come. He's dead. Gone. He is no longer.

ANGELA: What ceremony is going on here?

(Embarrassed.)

Seems like a funeral.

ALBERTO: *(Approaches her. Measured and ceremonious.)*

I am so sorry. This way, please.

(The attendees clear her path. ALBERTO leads ANGELA to the cart.)

ANGELA: I was just passing by. I'm a tourist. Excuse me.

ALBERTO: The groom's mother. The groom's father. The bride.

ANGELA: Is this a funeral or a wedding?

(To herself.)

I don't know what's going on.

ALBERTO: Dear Amatsia Hofstadter...

BIANCA: Still – a crook.

ALBERTO: Today we bid you farewell.

GRAVEDIGGER: Righteousness shall go before Him...

(Pulls the cart and exits with it.)

LOLA: *(To ANGELA.)*

Come, come. You're in now. In deep.

(ALBERTO wraps his arm around ANGELA's shoulder. She wriggles free.)

ANGELA: I'm sorry. I'm just on vacation.

LOLA: What 'vacation'? What do you think over there in America?! Here people die! It's not America here! When the time comes to weep you'll also be saying vacation!

(Everyone exits apart from ANGELA. AVNER lingers for a moment, then leaves as well with his little trolley. ANGELA turns to leave. ELHANAN enters behind her.)

ELHANAN: Are you leaving?

ANGELA: Why, of course.

ELHANAN: I was his friend, you know.

ANGELA: What do you want?

ELHANAN: We can reminisce about him tonight.

ANGELA: About who?

ELHANAN: Amatsia, your fiancé.

ANGELA: Are you all crazy or what? They warned me that everyone's crazy in the Middle East!

(Exits.)

ELHANAN: *(To himself.)*

I thought that if I looked at her for a long time a miracle might happen and she'd suddenly be mine.

Act Thirteen

Night. In the street. ELHANAN stands, still deep in thought about ANGELA. The PROSTITUTE enters from the opposite side.

ELHANAN: *(To himself.)*

...and she'd suddenly be mine.

PROSTITUTE: I'm yours.

ELHANAN: *(Turns to her.)*

Not anymore.

(The PROSTITUTE approaches him, lifts up the hem of her dress.)

PROSTITUTE: No?

(ELHANAN is consumed by lust. He looks at her thighs.)

Eh?

(She wiggles her hips a little. ELHANAN moves towards her while shaking his head. Stops in front of her, get down on his knees.)

So why the talk, eh?

(ELHANAN kisses her thighs once, twice, succumbs to his passion, tries to hug her thighs, the PROSTITUTE slips away, drops the hem of her dress. ELHANAN chases after her on his knees, she pushes him away.)

Money.

ELHANAN: All my savings are for the trip.

(The PROSTITUTE lifts the hem of her dress in front of him and laughs. ELHANAN takes some money out of his pocket, gives it to her, kisses and hugs her thighs.)

PROSTITUTE: You'll be mine until you die or until you're broke, whichever comes first.

(ELHANAN embraces her thighs more vigorously. HENIA enters the street wearing breeches and a Turkish fez, an iron chain at her feet.)

HENIA: Elhanan, my son, I've been kidnapped by the Turkish sultan.

ELHANAN: *(Horrified, buries his face in the prostitute's thigh.)*

Mum!!

PROSTITUTE: Give me another five hundred! You're having a great time down there! Acting out your fantasies on my legs! Give me another five hundred!

HENIA: Son, I'm being taken to a brothel in Istanbul. The young Turkish men are waiting for me. I've been warning you all these years. Goodbye.

(Starts walking away slowly, as though being dragged against her will.)

ELHANAN: Mum! No! Wait for me, Mum!

PROSTITUTE: Give me another five hundred! Give it to me!

(ELHANAN empties his pockets, gives her everything, clings to her thighs in shame, buries his head in them.)

ELHANAN: Mummy...mummy...

HENIA: We'll all meet in Istanbul...

(She exits. Pause. ELHANAN removes his head from the PROSTITUTE's thighs. Checks his pockets, they're empty. The PROSTITUTE looks at him indifferently.)

PROSTITUTE: Filthy fantasies, spoiling my legs.

(She exits. ZIGGY enters with BOBEH's suitcase.)

ELHANAN: Travelling?

ZIGGY: G...g...g...grandma escaped from the institution a week ago. They found the suitcase ou...ou...outside town.

ELHANAN: And her?

ZIGGY: Th…th…th…this is what they f…found. The suitcase.

(ZIGGY exits. HENIA enters and stands at the window of her house. ELHANAN approaches in the street.)

ELHANAN: Mum.

HENIA: It's three in the morning, you bank robber.

ELHANAN: Mum, Mum!

HENIA: What are you so happy about, eh?

ELHANAN: I had a daydream…

HENIA: Where I die, of course! Going out at night to I-don't-even-want-say-where! Disgraceful! Money which should have been saved up for a flat! A flat! Elhanan, I'm warning you, this time I'm still alive, but next time…

(Shakes her head gravely.)

Yes, once upon a time there was also a Henia.

(Her eyes tear up.)

Ay, Henia, Henia.

ELHANAN: *(Hugs his mother, starts dancing with her.)*

Mum, Mum, I'm so happy you're here!

HENIA: You don't even know how to appreciate it! You should have had a mother who goes with the Turks to Istanbul!

ELHANAN: Istanbul!?

(To himself.)

You can't hide anything from the old woman, not even your dreams.

Act Fourteen

Night-time in the night club. MOTKE TZHORI is dancing with TZIPORA.

TZIPORA: You're totally crazy. You're insane.

MOTKE: So what if we go out to a night club for once? For once let's forget about the money, have a good time.

TZIPORA: Oh, you're a pig. Oh, you're a pig.

MOTKE: Why am I a pig?

TZIPORA: Why is he a pig. You don't know what it means to run a household.

MOTKE: How about we forget household management for half an hour?

TZIPORA: Forget?! Do you have any idea how much a pair of baby shoes costs these days? You're talking nonsense. You're a pig.

MOTKE: Do you want to go back home?

TZIPORA: Why did we come in here in the first place then?! How much did it cost to get in?

MOTKE: Seven hundred.

TZIPORA: You see? You see this pig? Seven hundred lira. In order to fully enjoy the seven hundred lira I'm going to have to dance until two in the morning, my uterus will drop out and you won't have any more descendants, we're done with the Tzhori dynasty.

(Sweeps him off to dance. They exit. BELLA and ALBERTO PINKUS dance in.)

BELLA: I don't believe that you really see something you like in me.

ALBERTO: Everything your mother has, plus youth.

BELLA: Do me a favour and don't mention the black widow, eh?

ALBERTO: From now on – only you.

BELLA: I'm looking at you and asking myself what you've got which is so appealing to women.

ALBERTO: I'm from South America.

BELLA: Tell me something about yourself.

ALBERTO: In my mind's eye I saw my life differently. People crowding around me in order to shake my hand. And here I am looking around me – no crowding! Loads of free space.

BELLA: They say you have a big cock.

(ALBERTO smiles a mysterious smile.)

I'm warning you Alberto, I'm not my mother.

(ALBERTO presses her against him and kisses her passionately on the mouth. BELLA pushes him away, shaking with lust.)

How dare…!

(Presses against him.)

Alberto take me to a faraway island!

ALBERTO: All right. We'll stop at my place on the way, I live just around the corner.

(They dance out. ZIGGY and ALPHONSE HUZLI, a young and dandily dressed man, dance in.)

ALPHONSE: Everyone's trying to narrow your horizons, to put you in a box. And I'm a person who tries to express himself.

ZIGGY: I feel that I also have a need to e...e...e...express myself.

ALPHONSE: I have a puppy at home. Eats like a baby. Suckles. So cute – fantastic. I bought a little hat for his tail.

ZIGGY: A poo...poo...poo...poodle?

ALPHONSE: A mini poodle. Want to see him? He'll be very happy.

ZIGGY: Why not.

(They dance out. Old BOBEH enters the street, her clothes torn and dirty, a bundle of rags in her hand. She crosses the road slowly. The sun rises, the light turns to dusk. BOBEH exits. The GRAVEDIGGER enters, pulling a cart carrying the body of ALBERTO PINKUS wrapped in a sheet. Behind it walk BIANCA, LOLA and BELLA all dressed in black, HENIA, ELHANAN, ZIGGY, ALPHONSE, BRUNO, TZILA, MOTKE, TZIPORA and AVNER with a trolley with a suitcase on it. The funeral procession comes to a stop.)

GRAVEDIGGER: Vi izder eulogizer?[1]

LOLA: *(Points at ALBERTO's corpse.)*

Du.[2]

GRAVEDIGGER: Oy vey. Righteousness shall go before Him...

(Pulls the cart behind him, exits, followed by everyone else apart from AVNER, MOTKE and TZIPORA.)

AVNER: The last suitcase.

1 [Yiddish] Where is the eulogizer?
2 [Yiddish] There.

TZIPORA: Who knows.

AVNER: It really is.

MOTKE: All right. I understand we're saying goodbye.

AVNER: I'm going to live not far away.

TZIPORA: I'm not going to be handing out dinners.

MOTKE: Tzipora, let me say goodbye to my brother properly.

TZIPORA: You understand? Saying goodbye! The Tzhori brothers are going to kiss each other, the Tzhori brothers are going to wave each other with silk handkerchiefs.

MOTKE: Why do you have to spoil everything, Tzipora?

TZIPORA: I'm spoiling?! Was it you who washed your son's nappies?! Fat Tzhori and hunchback Tzhori are saying goodbye. I spoil everything!

(She exits. MOTKE wants to say something nice to AVNER, but now isn't able to.)

MOTKE: All right, calm down.

AVNER: If you want to visit sometimes...

MOTKE: She's my wife. She's done a lot for me, she's made me into a human being. I could have been a nobody, without any sense of belonging. I owe her a lot, I love her. Calm down.

(He exits. AVNER exits as well with his trolley. BRUNO enters with a suitcase and a bunch of flowers. TZILA enters after him.)

TZILA: Where to, Bruno?

BRUNO: I'm going to visit Amatsia, our son.

TZILA: What's the suitcase for?

BRUNO: *(Stares for a moment at the suitcase.)*

But...I'm going. To visit our son. The house is so empty and I...

(Pause.)

...want to be with my boy.

TZILA: I'm coming with you, Bruno, wait for me.

(She hugs him. He rests his head on her shoulder and sobs. She rocks him to calm him down and without him noticing also starts crying. They start walking with her still rocking him from side to side and him also rocking her in a kind of dance similar to the one they once danced with AMATSIA.)

BRUNO: Thirty years ago there was a ceremony...

TZILA: A man and a woman got married...

BRUNO: A year later they had a son...

TZILA: They gave him all their love...

BRUNO: The child grew up...

TZILA: They grew old...

BRUNO: And the child remained their only hope...

TZILA: Their only hope....

BRUNO: Their only hope...

(They exit. BIANCA, LOLA and BELLA enter wearing black, arm in arm.)

BIANCA: The best thing to do is learn learn bridge.

BELLA: We're missing a hand.

LOLA: Isn't Tzila Hofstadter going to be burying someone?

(They exit.)

Act Fifteen

Evening. Bus stop. ZIGGY enters with a suitcase, followed by ELHANAN.

ELHANAN: Going to the Sea of Galilee in the autumn?

ZIGGY: I've always loved the Sea of Galilee. And after that maybe I'll go abroad.

(ELHANAN lets out an impressed whistle.)

ELHANAN: Ziggy, Ziggy, who'd have imagined.

ZIGGY: This place is small, you see. A box. Abroad no one looks inside…your trousers.

(Pause.)

Look, I'm not leaving the country for political reasons. I've just found my happiness. Look, ever since I can remember myself I've stuttered, now – it's all gone.

(ALPHONSE HUZLI enters wearing a colourful blazer and a pretty leather bag, pulling a puppy on a leash behind him.)

ALPHONSE: The cashier says it's a three-hour trip.

ZIGGY: Meet a friend of mine, Elhanan. Alphonse.

(ELHANAN and ALPHONSE shake hands.)

ELHANAN: Nice to meet you.

ALPHONSE: How do you do.

(To ZIGGY.)

That's our bus, we need to get on.

(ZIGGY shakes ELHANAN's hand.)

ZIGGY: So long.

ELHANAN: Good luck.

(ALPHONSE wraps his arm around ZIGGY's back, walks while holding him. Before they exit, ZIGGY turns his head towards ELHANAN who's standing and looking at them. ZIGGY's face betrays embarrassment and helplessness. He exits with ALPHONSE. ELHANAN remains, standing. Pause. To himself.)

Everyone's going. Everyone's in motion. All I need to do is also pick up a suitcase and go to her. Show up there one evening, in the autumn, knock on the door, she'll open it surprised, hold her body to mine…and laugh about all the time we've been apart, all this long time we've been apart.

(Starts crying quietly.)

Why can't I have one day without missing her? One day without missing her. I don't have any more strength. I'm only human, I need to get my share, I need just one hour of rest alone with my share.

(AVNER TZHORI comes out onto the balcony of his new home in his pyjamas. ELHANAN stops crying, blows his nose.)

AVNER: What's wrong, Elhanan?

ELHANAN: How are you, Avner? How's the new flat?

AVNER: I'm warm, I'm fine.

(The PROSTITUTE enters, stands off to the side.)

PROSTITUTE: How come we don't see you any more, you lovely invalid.

AVNER: *(Laughs.)*

My age is having a favourable effect on my wallet: Twice a month is enough for me these days.

PROSTITUTE: Gentlemen, I'm not bringing forth bread from here, gentlemen.

ELHANAN: I'll come with you. I still need four times a month. Good night, Avner.

AVNER: Good night.

(To himself.)

In three-four years, I reckon, once a year will be enough for me. Once a year, the first night of spring, cravings, savings.

(BIANCA, BELLA and LOLA enter wearing black.)

BIANCA: Good evening, Mr Tzhori, congratulations on the new flat. There's a bridge group getting together and we're missing a hand.

AVNER: Yes, I am a man with free time, and I'll happily give my hand.

LOLA: So hurry up and get dressed, what are you waiting for, and come to learn the fundamentals of bridge with Mrs Schuster.

AVNER: One minute, I'm coming.

(He exits. LOLA starts quietly singing a rude song.)

LOLA: *(Sings.)*

Cucumber green and wide,
Come fill me deep inside,
Tickle me there, tickle me here –
And come out with a reddish smear.

(BIANCA laughs.)

BIANCA: Why are you sad, Bella?

(AVNER enters the street, clothed.)

Are we off?

AVNER: I'm completely clueless about bridge.

(They start walking, except BELLA.)

BIANCA: What's wrong, Bella?

BELLA: Don't count my hand in.

BIANCA: But what's happened to you?

BELLA: *(Suddenly in an emotional tone.)*

Yes, you've already been through everything, you've already managed to get widowed, everything's behind you, I haven't even...haven't even...

(Almost crying, stops, shouts.)

I'm not going to waste my nights playing bridge with hunchbacks!!

(Pause.)

LOLA: Of course, Alberto Pinkus *was* Alberto Pinkus.

(Pause. AVNER comes up to BELLA. Quietly.)

AVNER: Bella, I've already forgotten about you, believe me. I don't even dream any more. I'm already totally, absolutely totally over it.

BELLA: Thank you very much. Even he isn't dreaming about me any more.

AVNER: Why did you call me? I was warm and happy on my balcony. Why did you take me away from there? What have I ever done to you? I'd almost gone to sleep to dream about French ladies, what have I ever done to you?

(Exits.)

BIANCA: Bella...

(BELLA runs out.)

Bella! Anyway, she should calm down. What were you saying earlier about Alberto Pinkus?

LOLA: I said that after all Alberto Pinkus was Alberto Pinkus.

BIANCA: Well, you would certainly know.

(They exit.)

Act Sixteen

The street in the early evening. The GRAVEDIGGER enters, pulling a cart carrying the body of BRUNO HOFSTADTER. Behind it walks TZILA who's sobbing loudly, behind her BIANCA, BELLA and LOLA wearing black, ELHANAN, HENIA, MOTKE, TZIPORA who's pregnant again, and AVNER. The GRAVEDIGGER is singing quietly to himself.

LOLA: He's starting to feel at home, the gravedigger.

(The GRAVEDIGGER stops in front of the HOFSTADTER residence. Long pause. Suddenly MOTKE clears his throat, then another long pause, after which.)

MOTKE: Dear Bruno Hofstadter.

(Pause.)

Today we bid you farewell,

(Pause.)

GRAVEDIGGER: Righteousness...

MOTKE: After we only recently bid farewell to your son.

GRAVEDIGGER: Righteousness...

MOTKE: Rest in peace, Bruno Hofstadter, in this neighbourhood you'll be remembered as a decent man, devoted to his family, his friends, and above all – to his people.

BIANCA: Bravo, Mr Tzhori!

LOLA: Did you see that?

BIANCA: That's how leaders emerge. Suddenly. Spontaneously.

MOTKE: *(Emotional, shakes the hands of all the people gathering around him.)*

I myself don't know how suddenly...suddenly I just... suddenly I felt...I really...well, I think I owe a lot to my wife.

TZIPORA: Don't get too excited, Motke, it's not a relative, it's a neighbour.

LOLA: The new Alberto. Yes, the new Alberto! The new Alberto!

TZIPORA: *(In a sharp, high voice.)*

I'll show you the new Alberto in a second, Mrs Globchik!

(Moves towards her threateningly.)

MOTKE: Friends...friends, let us not forget...

(Motions to the GRAVEDIGGER to keep walking.)

GRAVEDIGGER: Righteousness shall go before Him...

(Pulls the cart and exits. Everyone exits after him. BIANCA, BELLA, TZILA and LOLA enter, all wearing black and arm in arm.)

BIANCA: A fourth hand.

(They exit. The light fades. Night. Old BOBEH crosses the road slowly, her clothes tattered and torn, her face and hair caked with mud, in her hand is a bundle of rags and newspapers. She exits. ELHANAN enters, stands at the station, takes some money out of his pocket, counts it, puts it back in his pocket, waits. The PROSTITUTE comes in wearing travel gear, a coat, and carrying a suitcase in her hand.)

ELHANAN: You too?

PROSTITUTE: To Switzerland.

(She pronounces 'Switzerland' like 'S-why-tzerland'.)

ELHANAN: What?!

PROSTITUTE: Didn't you hear? Switzerland. Obviously. Here one person'll come twice a month, another one four times a month, and my talent goes to waste. I'm fighting against time, aren't I? In Switzerland, dear sir, it's horniness. Yes, they're pink, they have pink houses, they have pink skin, but sir the horniness. The Swiss man says 'Bitte Bitte', I fart in his ear, and he's willing to pay a lot of money for that. Obviously.

ELHANAN: She took everything I'd saved for going to Switzerland, and now she's going to Switzerland.

PROSTITUTE: Obviously. While you're banging – I'm planning. Even now. Goodbye, good sir, if you come to Switzerland, you'll work for me selling falafel.

(She exits. ELHANAN sits at the station. The sun comes up. Dawn. BELLA enters with a suitcase, and BIANCA is with her.)

BELLA: Goodbye, Elhanan, I'm going.

ELHANAN: Going? Am I ever going to stop hearing the word 'going', 'going'?

BIANCA: Guess where. To London. To study international relations. We have relatives there. Stiglitz, maybe you remember them, they'll arrange a part time job for her working with children.

BELLA: That's it Mum, I don't want you to walk me any further.

BIANCA: I want to go to the airport, Bellinka. What'll people say, that a mother isn't...

BELLA: Bellinka isn't moving another inch unless you go back home.

63

BIANCA: What have I done to you? To all of you! Why are you leaving me to die?! I'm all alone, have you thought about that?! I dedicated my entire life to all of you...

(Laughs.)

Children! A husband and children! You interrupted my rummy and bridge games! Interruptions in my rummy game, that's what you were! Go! Scatter in the air! Go!

(She exits. Pause.)

BELLA: Not that I'm under any illusions about London. London isn't waiting for me. I'll be alone there too, and maybe this time it's for life – being alone. But in London there are more films on, good music, excellent television, more courteous people, so that the despair becomes more comfortable. You understand? If I'm going to end up like a dog, at least let the television be proper television. Goodbye.

(She exits. Pause.)

ELHANAN: *(To himself.)*

Everyone's gone.

Act Seventeen

Night. The street. Old BOBEH crosses the road very slowly. Before exiting she stumbles, carries on for another step or two, falls, crawls off. A VOICE calls out from offstage:

A VOICE: The hunchback's killed himself! The hunchback's hung himself! The hunchback's killed himself! The hunchback's hung himself!

(Lights come on inside the houses. Men and women in pyjamas go out onto their balconies, stand in the windows. MOTKE TZHORI runs into the street, wearing his pyjamas, followed by the pregnant TZIPORA with a baby in her arms. MOTKE is agitated and sweating, he doesn't say a thing, but looks at the people in the houses around him. TZIPORA tries to pull him home, he doesn't respond, paces to and fro, once in a while lets out a moan of someone who's about to burst into tears, but he doesn't cry, just mumbles to himself.)

MOTKE: Little brother with a hunchback…little brother with a hunchback…

(And suddenly he stops, his body goes limp. TZIPORA goes to him and walks him away without any resistance. One by one the neighbours clear away from the balconies and from the windows, lights turn off. ELHANAN and HENIA stay at the window. ELHANAN is drinking a lot of water from a bottle.)

HENIA: Don't forget that I can also hang myself one day, it's not a problem for me, don't forget that.

ELHANAN: *(Stops drinking.)*

Here's the window, open it and jump – you're free, I'm free.

HENIA: Who said I wasn't?

(Approaches the window.)

Do I have a lot to lose? Do I have anything? Am I alive?

(Leans over the window.)

Is there anything waiting for me apart from a heart attack and a funeral?

(Looks down. Pause.)

ELHANAN: Loves herself.

HENIA: That's not true, I hate myself! I hate myself! The world doesn't want me! The world has vomited me! Just let me die!

(She looks down. Pause, turns away from the window.)

Let me die, let me die, let me die…

(Exits crying. ELHANAN drinks some more water and exits as well. The sun comes up. Evening. The GRAVEDIGGER enters pulling a cart carrying BOBEH GLOBCHIK's body covered with a sheet. Behind her walks no one. MOTKE enters the street, sweating, breathing heavily.)

MOTKE: The traffic…

(Wipes the sweat from his face, starts walking in measured steps behind the cart. In front of him enters another GRAVEDIGGER, pulling a cart carrying the body of AVNER TZHORI covered with a sheet, and which also has no one walking behind it. MOTKE gets confused, stares in embarrassment at the cart he's following and at the cart coming opposite, approaches the GRAVEDIGGER he's following, and asks quietly.)

MOTKE: Excuse me, who's passed away here?

GRAVEDIGGER: A lady. Globchik.

MOTKE: Oy.

(Runs after the second cart which has passed by in the meantime, to the SECOND GRAVEDIGGER.)

Do you by any chance have a hunchback?

SECOND GRAVEDIGGER: Yes, I've got everything.

(MOTKE follows that cart. The first one's left in the meantime. This one, with MOTKE behind it, exits too. The light dims. Night. ZIGGY enters with a suitcase in his hand, arrives at his house. LOLA comes out to greet him, wearing a night gown, her hair wrapped in a net and her face covered in cream.)

ZIGGY: Pi...pi...pi...pi...

(Pause.)

Pi...pi...pi...pi...

(Experiences a sharp tic across his head and shoulders. Pause.)

Pi...pi...

LOLA: All right, Ziggy. Speak tomorrow.

ZIGGY: *(Another tic.)*

Pi...pi...pi...pi...

(Pause.)

Pi...pi...

LOLA: But come inside now, Ziggy, it's night time.

ZIGGY: Pi...pi...

LOLA: Tell me tomorrow.

ZIGGY: Today. Pi...pi...pi...

(LOLA strokes his head, he pulls away, has another tic.)

Pi...pi...pi...pi...

(Walks into the middle of the street, struggles to speak while experiencing the sharp tic across his head and shoulders.)

Pi...pi...pi...pi...

(Neighbours come out onto their balconies, watch him struggle.)

LOLA: My son's back, he wants to say something.

ZIGGY: Pi...pi...pi...pi...

NEIGHBOURS: *(Start helping him.)*

Pi...pi...pi...pi...

ZIGGY: Pi...pi...pi...pi...

(The volume of the neighbours rises. A choir forms.)

NEIGHBOURS: Pi...pi...pi...pi...

ZIGGY: *(His voice rises above everyone else's, he writhes, his face red with effort.)*

Pi...pi...pi...pi...

(And with a mighty shout and final exertion.)

Pigs!!

(Absolute silence descends. Pause. ZIGGY exits proudly.)

LOLA: That's what my son's like, he's always spoken his mind.

(People return to their rooms. Lights go out. LOLA and BIANCA stay behind.)

BIANCA: What about Ziggy for a fourth hand?

LOLA: He doesn't have the head for it. But we'll find someone. We're the life force of this neighbourhood. We won't die, we'll play bridge. We'll end up representing this neighbourhood, our dead husbands, our children, all our lives, we'll end up representing them at bridge.

(Exit.)

Act Eighteen

Night. Street. TWO PARAMEDICS enter, carrying a stretcher on which lies HENIA GELERNTER, her head slightly raised. ELHANAN is walking alongside the stretcher.

ELHANAN: So that's how it is, one evening, with no advance notice…

HENIA: Exactly how I told you it would happen. Mummy promises – Mummy delivers.

ELHANAN: There's still something we need to discuss.

HENIA: I was like a little sneeze to you. You say 'bless you' and move on.

(The PARAMEDICS exit with the stretcher. ELHANAN remains.)

ELHANAN: *(Perhaps to himself, perhaps to HENIA who's left.)*

We still haven't clarified what needs to be clarified. All the important topics are still on the agenda. We still haven't said anything to each other. We need to talk, Mum, we still need to talk.

(Pause. To himself.)

And I was acting like we had all of eternity ahead of us.

(The sun rises. Early evening. The GRAVEDIGGER enters, pulling a cart carrying HENIA GELERNTER's body covered with a sheet. Behind her walk BIANCA, LOLA, ZIGGY, TZILA, MOTKE and TZIPORA. The funeral procession stops in front of the GELERNTER residence. MOTKE walks up to ELHANAN who's standing away from the group, puts his hand on his shoulder, leads him towards the funeral congregation, then stands in front of everyone, ready to eulogize.)

MOTKE: Today we bid farewell to Henia Gelernter. What can we say about her? That she was a humble woman. Decent. What else? Devoted to her family and her son. She never bothered any of us, lived her life quietly. Relatively quietly, of course. Because in the ears of those closest to her she always complained of aches and illnesses. But apart from that, total quiet. Not a sound. She leaves no trace. And I ask myself what you might also be asking yourselves. Surely apart from the fear of diseases there must have been something more to her, things which went unsaid, a life which went unlived. After all we didn't come into this world in order to complain about diseases. We also didn't come into the world to count money. And we didn't come into the world to play bridge.

BIANCA: I can't see that we're playing any bridge yet.

MOTKE: Nevertheless, the actual thing we need to say still isn't being said. And so I ask: after everything, when we're lying here on this cart, and the white sheet is covering us, and soon the earth will cover us as well, when we're lying here everything suddenly becomes very clear, what was wheat and what was chaff, it's clear to us that there was something else to say which we didn't say, we wasted, we chewed and we spat out, and we didn't say it. Lord, you gave us funerals to remind us of our lives, please make sure we don't forget this cart and this sheet between the funerals too.

LOLA: *(Crying quietly.)*

That's so moving…so true…

BIANCA: *(Joins in the crying.)*

Shabtai, Shabtai…

TZIPORA: Motke's started reading philosophy and goes to synagogue every morning.

70

MOTKE: Quiet, Tzipora.

TZIPORA: And wait and see what he'll have prepared for you for next time.

GRAVEDIGGER: Righteousness shall go before Him...

(Pulls the cart, exits, all the others follow him out. The light fades, evening arrives. ELHANAN enters the street with a suitcase, walks towards the bus stop. Behind him enter his father TZVI and his mother HENIA dressed like tourists, arm in arm, smiling.)

HENIA: Elhanan.

(ELHANAN stops, turns his head towards them.)

ELHANAN: Mum. Dad.

TZVI: Come and watch panoramic cinema in the sky, Elhanan.

HENIA: Dad as usual with the frivolous spending – America, cinema, ice cream! You've also got just the view which is free, good air. Come walk with us Elhanan.

ELHANAN: I'm going to Switzerland.

HENIA: We'll walk above Switzerland too.

ELHANAN: *(Crying.)*

And when will I live in Switzerland itself.

(ELHANAN looks outside for a moment, in the direction of the bus stop, then gives up, puts the suitcase down, sits on it. The light fades, night comes. The sun slowly rises. The TWO HASIDIC JEWS hurry by on their way to the synagogue while mumbling.)

HASIDIC JEWS: I give thanks before you, King living and eternal, for You have returned within me my soul with compassion; abundant is Your faithfulness!

(From different corners emerge NINA, ELISHA HOOKER, BELLA, ZIGGY, ANGELA HOPKINS and ALPHONSE HUZLI, all carrying suitcases. They stand silently next to their suitcases.)

HENIA: Come, child, come and walk with your mother and father.

ELHANAN: Everyone who's stood between me and death has died. Nothing separates me from death any more.

HENIA: Come, Elhanan.

ELHANAN: Soon, soon.

(AVNER TZHORI enters with a little trolley with a suitcase on it, behind him is BOBEH with her little suitcase, both of them dressed like tourists, walking along happy and contented.)

AVNER: The final suitcase.

ELHANAN: I'll come soon.

END

THE LOST WOMEN OF TROY

A play based on Euripides

Translated from the Hebrew by Naaman Tammuz

Following the Greek tragedy *The Trojan Women* by Euripides, Levin tells the story of the ultimate victims of the great ancient war, the women and children that were left behind. In Levin's play, there are no gods and no mercy, only sorrow, pain and suffering. Troy is already burned to ashes, the great Greek victory has been achieved, but violence is still the only way of life.

Cast of Characters

AGAMEMNON, *king of Argos, commander-in-chief of the Greek army*

ODYSSEUS, *king of Ithaca, a commander in the Greek army*

MENELAUS, *king of Sparta, a commander in the Greek army*

NEOPTOLEMUS, *king of Thessaly, a commander in the Greek army*

TALTHYBIUS, *an adjutant in the Greek army*

HECUBA, *queen of Troy, prisoner of the Greek army*

CASSANDRA, *daughter of Hecuba, prisoner of the Greek army*

ANDROMACHE, *Hecuba's daughter-in-law, prisoner of the Greek army*

ASTYANAX, *son of Andromache, a child, prisoner of the Greek army*

HELEN, *wife of Menelaus, prisoner of the Greek army*

GREEK SOLDIERS

FEMALE PRISONERS FROM TROY

The play takes place in the Greek camp, near the ruins of the city of Troy. The female prisoners from Troy are brought before the assembled Greek commanders.

Premiere	The Cameri Theatre, Tel Aviv, 1984
Director	Hanoch Levin
Costume and Stage Design	Roni Toren
Lighting Design	Brian Harris
Music Composition	Foldi Shatz

Cast:

AGAMEMNON	Yossef Carmon
ODYSSEUS	Yonathan Tchertchi
MENELAUS	Yitshak Hizkia
NEOPTOLEMUS	Dov Glikman
TALTHYBIUS	Albert Cohen
HECUBA	Zaharira Harifai
CASSANDRA	Rivka Noiman
ANDROMACHE	Geta Munte
ASTYANAX	Yehudit Yanai
HELEN	Fabiana Meyuhas
FEMALE PRISONER 1	Ronit Ofir
FEMALE PRISONER 2	Hani Nachmias
FEMALE PRISONER 3	Hanna Pik

Chapter One: The Lamentation

NEOPTOLEMUS: The great artist up above is calmly sketching the final lines
    into the picture of war: a column of smoke rising above a demolished house,
    a dress rolling in the dust, a woman, her hair in disarray,
    being shoved by a soldier into the town square.

Here too is a dog busying itself with the entrails
of a rotting human corpse.
The picture is perfectly complete.

And the women come and gather here in the square.
Women, women, the sweet, suffocating moisture,
from which grow all the poisonous mushrooms of our soul.

Hecuba, wife of king Priam of Troy,
as of this morning his widow; mother of Hector and Paris,
the heroic princes, as of this morning their bereaved mother;
mistress of the kingdoms, glory of the world, as of this morning
a small filthy puddle of tears,
the spit of a beggar by the wayside.

Hecuba's daughter, Cassandra. They say of that crazy woman
that she is gifted with prophetic powers. Cassandra, what will be my fate?

(CASSANDRA remains silent.)

Nothing. Sees the future, no doubt.

Hecuba's daughter-in-law, Andromache. Wife of Hector,

as of this morning his widow. This morning has not been auspicious
for the married. She has a young child, Astyanax.
Yesterday he still had a future; today he is simply the owner of a past.
Five years old, and his main occupation is – reminiscing.

Helen, beautiful Helen, the raisin in the cake, the one
who caused all this, wife of Menelaus of Sparta
who is sitting here with us, betrayed her husband with Paris,
ran away with him to Troy, refused to return, and because of whom
Menelaus gathered all his allies, and with king Agamemnon in command
attacked Troy to raze her to the ground;
For this was not a matter of politics, but only of honour.
Helen's face, the face that launched a thousand ships,
by nightfall today will have launched, I'm afraid, but a worm.

And other women, women, court princesses, distinguished ladies,
all bereaved and freshly widowed, hot,
the grand prize for the victorious army's soldiers.

Hey, ladies, get used to being another body's shadow,
get used to being one of those for whom the world was not created.

Now the fire rises and intensifies. The city is in flames.
There is no Troy, ladies and gentlemen. Officially: Gone.
The picture is complete.
Stand, Hecuba – it is time to mourn.

HECUBA: Indeed, victorious commanders of Greece, you
have had

a handsome meal, it's time for the compote. And we are your compote.

And you, polished and neat officer of ceremonies, waiter of wars,
perhaps you also have advice for me on how to begin my lamentation?
With the smoke rising above my palace in Troy,
dissipating into the reddening skies along with my entire life?
With Priam my dead husband? With my two sons who were meant, when the time came, to carry their father to his grave, but are now being buried on the same day as him? Or with my daughters and daughter-in-law who are imprisoned
here with me, and from between whose legs blood and the semen of drunken
soldiers will flow tonight, 'the grand prize', as you called them?

And maybe I'll begin with what the future holds for me? To whom will you
give me as a servant? On what foreign shore am I to be discarded,
me, a queen and a lady? And what will my master be like?
Will he beat me? Will he humiliate me? And on the doorstep
of which lady's room will I loiter, waiting to be
summoned to put on her sandals, to attend to her body,
a decrepit, creaking slave, an old piece of furniture?

PRISONER A: And me? A final glance at the faces of my dead children, and then
into whose bed? My lips, which kissed the curls of the baby

that I have lost, will be buried in the pubic hair of a drunken Greek!...

PRISONER B: Why are you crying? What are they going to do to us?

PRISONER A: Sssh, my child, they won't kill us, they'll just take us to another country, far away: I'm crying for home...

PRISONER B: If we're to be exiled – then let it be to Athens; Its streets, so I've heard,
are paved with gold, and its temples are immense;
If I am to be a slave – at least I'll see the world.

PRISONER C: And I have brought some rouge and blue eye shadow with me, the provisions of a woman who's going out into the world;
Girls, learn to walk jauntily, these are your weapons: a perky breast, swaying buttocks, an inviting smile...

PRISONER B: It won't be possible to make me forget my husband and my children all at once,
but with a patient man, if I get one, I'll forget them slowly.

PRISONER B: I'm scared! You said this was a dream!
This is a terrible dream, like I've never dreamt before...

PRISONER C: Smile...smile...

PRISONER B: When will I wake from it? When I cried out in my dreams,
Daddy always came and gathered me in his arms;
now here I am, screaming, shivering and sweating – where are Daddy's arms? When am I going to wake up?! When am I going to wake up?!

PRISONER C: Smile at the messenger, here he comes like a
  whore-house pimp,
  smile because the situation's too hopeless to cry about,
  save your tears for happy times.

Chapter Two: Dividing the spoils

TALTHYBIUS: Hecuba, I am Talthybius. I came to you once as an emissary

on behalf of the Greek army which was besieging Troy. You were a queen then.

We met in better times, perhaps it is best not to mention them,

for it is with neither light heart nor boastfulness that I regard you now in your disgrace:

What has happened to you stands as a flag and a symbol for the fate of us all.

Even the duty which I have now been tasked with is far from gladdening my heart.

I will be the one that informs each of you whose slave and mistress

you will be, and where you will be taken to.

PRISONERS: Where will we be taken? Where? Whose whores and slaves will we be?

HECUBA: There is tenderness and sensitivity in your words, Talthybius; were these also expressed to the military commanders? Did you ask for mercy for us?

TALTHYBIUS: No, Hecuba. I am a messenger. Feelings are a personal matter.

HECUBA: Yes, I remember now. A messenger. The obsequiousness and cowardice reminded me who you were straight away.

Finding favour with everyone – that's your natural state.

But first tell me what will be the fate of my daughter, Cassandra?

I worry for her more than anyone, she is a priestess of Apollo,
a virgin, gripped by a feverish madness; we'll all get by,
man is an adaptive creature, but Cassandra, she lives
in dark, distant worlds, akin to a baby.
What will become of my daughter Cassandra?

TALTHYBIUS: She has been given to Agamemnon.

HECUBA: A servant to his Spartan wife?! – ha, poor child!

TALTHYBIUS: To Agamemnon himself. More precisely, to his bed.
Cassandra will be his concubine.

HECUBA: She is consecrated to Apollo! No man would dare violate her chastity!

TALTHYBIUS: Apollo? Perhaps. Some demon has indeed taken hold of her,
but she has caught the eye of Agamemnon.
There are difficulties, but Agamemnon desires it.

Would you not praise her good fortune at being chosen to serve
in a king's bed? Consider how easy her work is.
She could instead have found herself hunched, over folding dirty sheets
at the crack of dawn. Instead, at the crack of dawn she will still be asleep,
her breasts pressed under the hands of a powerful patron.

She will be the one dirtying sheets, which other slaves,
uglier than her, will break their backs washing.

HECUBA: And my second daughter, Polyxena, the one you separated me from?

To whose bed is Polyxena going?

TALTHYBIUS: To Achilles' tombstone.

HECUBA: His tombstone?

TALTHYBIUS: To watch over it.

HECUBA: What's that? Some Greek custom I'm not familiar with?

TALTHYBIUS: Be silent. Your daughter is silent too.

HECUBA: What do you mean 'silent'? Is she alive?!

TALTHYBIUS: She is free from suffering, her worries are over.

HECUBA: And Andromache my daughter-in-law? Wife of Hector my son,
to whom is she being given?

TALTHYBIUS: She has been chosen by the son of Achilles, Neoptolemus.

HECUBA: And me, all wrinkles and grey hair, no longer fit for someone's bed, what will become of me?

TALTHYBIUS: A slave to Odysseus. King of Ithaca.

HECUBA: Aah! To Odysseus!
To the highway robber Odysseus! The petty thief Odysseus,
who makes a mockery of all law and order, who turns every blossoming garden
into scorched earth, traitor, murderer, born liar…

ODYSSEUS: *(Strikes her.)*
Be careful, old bitch. Gone are the days when you could say anything that crossed your mind. Learn to filter your thoughts,
to say only nice things to your master, how handsome,

84

how right he his. Learn to shut up. Learn to serve in
silence.
Surely you can see: there is no trace left of your status.
Even your age
counts for nothing. Nothing counts for anything. Nothing.

HECUBA: To you the riches and the power, to you the youth,
and to me the cold and the anguish.
It is your turn to stand on top of the world, kicking,
my turn to fall into the abyss.

PRISONERS: And us? Us? Who are we going to be given to?

TALTHYBIUS: I will answer truthfully. Your future isn't exactly
looking rosy:
You will each in turn, one by one, be given
to the military men, to bend your backs or spread your legs,
all according to the wishes of your new masters.

If you have a spark in your eye and an alluring breast, you
will be mistresses.
Every night will see dirty waves of lust breaking against
your bodies.
And when your flesh is tattered and your breast is
squeezed dry,
you will drag yourselves from room to room, living
breathing rags, to carry out
the most humiliating household chores, until the day you die.
Then you will be thrown into a nameless pit, with no
gravestone, no tears.
Troy, this is the price of the end.

All of you, apart from you, Helen. You will die sooner.
At the end of this day you will die.

PRISONERS: Now! Kill the whore now!

A city and its inhabitants have been wiped out because of
a whore's smile;
Now it's time for the smile to get wiped out!
Kill the whore now!

TALTHYBIUS: At the end of the day, before the ships set sail,
at the hand of Menelaus
her betrayed husband. That is Menelaus' wish.

Chapter Three: Cassandra

AGAMEMNON: Now I want Cassandra. Dress
　　Cassandra up like a whore for me. Put sparkling clothes
　　on her,
　　decorate her with cheap trinkets. Make her pretty
　　in a commonplace kind of way; I've had my fill of
　　priestesses, give me whores!

CASSANDRA: Congratulate me. I am going to bed with a king.
　　You, mother, had to shed tears and mourn the death of my
　　father,
　　my murdered brothers and Troy which has gone up in
　　flames,
　　but now console yourself, because fortune has favoured
　　your daughter:
　　I am going to bed with a king!

　　Mother, forget your tragedies, dance! Dance and sing, my
　　sisters,
　　in honour of Cassandra: To bed with a king! With a king
　　to bed!

HECUBA: Aah, Cassandra my daughter, the terrible blow
　　which has been landed
　　on our heads hasn't cured your delirious mind:
　　You step towards the abyss of your humiliation with a
　　smile on your face.

CASSANDRA: With a smile on my face, mother, only with a
　　smile. To bed with a king. Because this king
　　will find me to be a far worse bride than Helen. Helen
　　sent you out
　　to war, Agamemnon; I will bring you back from it to
　　sevenfold

destruction and devastation. You are a victorious king, but
I am a whore of losers.

Come to my arms, Agamemnon. Your wife, like us, is now
making love

to the person you charged with protecting your home.
Between each moan of

pleasure and the next I hear them weaving the net of your
undoing.

You will die, hence the smile. And your son will murder
his mother

over your death, hence the smile. The entire house of
Atreus will be

wiped off the face of the earth. Come, come to my arms,
Agamemnon, because

there's another reason for it, for the smile:
When I come with you to Argos, I too will be murdered
along with you.
Aah, what a thorough bloodbath, one for which the ten-
year war
with Troy was merely the opening act! Hence,
Agamemnon, the smile!

HECUBA: Enough, my child! Be quiet! You get murdered here
for less than that!

AGAMEMNON: I believe you. I believe that the gods really do
speak from your mouth. From the day I sacrificially
slaughtered
my beloved daughter Iphigenia, and thousands of other
victims in exchange for this victory – somewhere out there
an axe was raised above my head; and all the rest – is just
a matter of time.

I am your sentence and you are mine, Cassandra. In this
embrace we are not

king and slave, but two branches cut from a tree
and thrown to the water, carried slowly downstream
towards the river's mouth.

CASSANDRA: Take me now, Agamemnon, quickly! On the
brink of death
I will celebrate my betrothal, my naked corpse will be
dumped beside your dismembered body...

Here she is, your wife, exiting the palace, her dress
already soaked with your blood, on her lips a horrific
deceitful smile,
behind her back the knife intended for me...

Yes, the knife is sharpened, I'm coming, I'll just remove
these priestly ornaments,
the robe, the bracelets, the scarves, the rings, what need
have I for all these,
the decorations have deceived me. If god only knows how
to take –
what use have we for a god; take, take this naked body
which hasn't yet been desecrated, and stain it with dirt and
blood...

Dear god, at least death will be easy, no twitching and
foaming,
the pulse will gently weaken until it comes to rest, like a
peaceful descent into sleep...

If so, why the fear, Cassandra? Everyone is dead,
dead, the city is destroyed, now it is your turn...

Ah, the decay, the decay, the stench of my flesh rotting in
a pit!...

No, no, it's not out of fear that I'm crying out now, but
only to remind

the witnesses: There was a girl, Cassandra, she never
lived!...

And outside the sun will still rise, the smell of the sea
is so sharp, and at night they will strum the kithara …

Mother, mother, we were born and made plans in vain,
in vain you fed me warm milk and tucked me in at night,
my life has been woven with no meaning, and now with
no meaning it is coming undone.

AGAMEMNON: 'In vain, in vain'! What, when regarded after
the passage of time, does not appear to be in vain?!
How meaningless it is to talk about meaninglessness!

CASSANDRA: Oh people, fate. The colours of happiness are
so intense,
and yet with the lightest touch, like the passing of a damp
cloth across a board,
the entire picture is erased; that, is what hurts so much.

MILITARY LEADERS: *(Sing.)*
In the sprawling killing fields we left many a brother and
friend,
oh men, the night has forever taken them away,
dust and scream have settled, and the world is at peace
again,
so many of us went, so few have returned today.

A woman's mourning song will help her baby into sleep
descend
waits another second, only her hair turns slowly grey;
In the sprawling killing fields we left many a brother and
friend,
oh men, the night has forever taken them away.

Chapter Four: Polyxena

HECUBA: Has the time also come for me to wear a sackcloth?
To start on the humiliating household chores? Bring me
the tools for wiping and scrubbing!
Where's the laundry tub? – I'll use it to drown the storm
in my heart!
Give me filthy underwear – a final act of kindness to the
Trojan monarchy!

Or perhaps, Odysseus, I should first wait to see
what fate will befall my second and last daughter,
Polyxena?
I still have my daughter Polyxena, what will you do with
her?

ANDROMACHE: Give Polyxena a rest, Hecuba. Give her a
rest just as she herself is resting.

HECUBA: I want to know what's going to happen to my
daughter Polyxena!

ANDROMACHE: Do you need it to be stated explicitly?! No
one can shape her fate now, because her fate is sealed, out
of the hands of mankind.

TALTHYBIUS: Polyxena was chosen to be slaughtered on the
grave of Achilles
in order to appease his spirit with the blood of the king of
Troy's daughter.
The angry spirit of Achilles would not allow us to
sail our ships away from here without this sacrifice.

HECUBA: Ah, Polyxena, Polyxena, you too have been
sentenced to die!

Murder upon murder upon murder, senseless and never-
ending!

Odysseus, I must ask you a question
before Polyxena's execution...

ANDROMACHE: Hecuba, Polyxena is dead!!

HECUBA: Not dead! Her fate hasn't been sealed yet!
Odysseus
was also made in the womb of a woman, he too is a father
to children,
Odysseus will listen to what I have to say to him first!

Odysseus, you owe me your life. Surely you remember
how you once came to spy on Troy. You disguised yourself
as a beggar.
You came in tattered clothes, your face caked in filth,
congealed blood on your tangled beard.

ODYSSEUS: I remember the incident. Its scars are etched into
my flesh.

HECUBA: But Helen saw through your disguise
and told me who you were. She told only me.

ODYSSEUS: Yes, I was in mortal danger.

HECUBA: How you stooped and grovelled on your knees to
beg for your life.

ODYSSEUS: My hand froze to the hem of your dress.

HECUBA: You were at my mercy. You were my slave then.
Do you also remember what you said to me?

ODYSSEUS: Said? Anything I could. Anything in order to stay
alive.

HECUBA: Yes, you certainly begged. And it was I who gave you
   your life. I set you free.

ODYSSEUS: Thanks to you I am alive.

HECUBA: Thanks to the mother's heart in my chest. As I looked down at you
   from above I saw my own son begging for his life.
   And that same mother's heart thanks to which you are standing here,
   is now breaking at your feet; Are you able to ignore it?

ANDROMACHE: Hecuba, it's too late!

HECUBA: Look into my eyes and answer me: Is this how you repay your debt to me?

   And perhaps you'll say that you personally would have done without this killing, but that the people demanded it?!
   Ah, the people, the people, whose opinion is never sought, and in whose name you, the statesmen,
   carry out the most vile criminal acts in the world!
   Is there a single despicable act which hasn't been perpetrated under the guise of being the will of the people?!

   And what excuses will you use to justify this death?!
   The war is over, the dead are lying in their eternal resting places,
   hasn't enough blood been spilled here on Trojan soil?!
   Aren't there enough dead in the world already without the death of Polyxena?!
   And the spirit of Achilles, hasn't it quenched its thirst with the blood of my husband and my sons?!

   Or perhaps you need yet more revenge, more blood,

if so, why Polyxena?! What's my daughter got to do with
the dead Achilles?!
Who has hurt him less, who has had less to do with the fate
of Achilles than my wretched daughter?!
If it's revenge you seek– take Helen!
You came to Troy because of her, she's the adulteress, demand
Achilles' blood from her! Kill Helen!

No, Odysseus, don't answer me, I'm not done yet,
I must get down on my knees before you as you did
before me; -
Here, on my knees, my hand frozen to the hem of your
clothes, like your
hand back then on the hem of my dress, I'm asking for my
compensation:
a life for a life.

Odysseus, everything I've lost lives on inside her,
she is the treasure of my memories, the Troy I have lost,
my family,
leave her for me just as a relic, a miserable souvenir in the
hands of a refugee…

And you have power, Odysseus, but your heart is
merciful!
You will not flaunt your power at an old, broken,
impoverished woman, this power will also pass one day,
look at me, take heed, in the space on an hour
Hecuba's glory has gone up in smoke, leaving behind only
an outstretched hand…

Agamemnon, you are the commander in chief, beside you
lies
my daughter Cassandra; What will you give me, master,
in return for your nights of love with her?
What reparations will she and I receive from you

for all the tenderness you will be receiving in bed? Prove that her
caresses are pleasurable to you and throw some
compensation my way…

Humans, listen to your hearts for once,
you are all fathers, you are all sons to mothers,
you will pardon her, oh military leaders of Greece, wise strategizers,
surely you will find one small crack in the great wall of death,
through which my daughter Polyxena can save her soul!
You won't kill my daughter Polyxena, you won't
kill my daughter Polyxena, you won't kill her!

ANDROMACHE: Hecuba, they have already killed her.

HECUBA: Killed?! Killed Polyxena?! Is this what you meant, Talthybius,
when you said to me 'She is free of suffering, she is silent,
her worries are over'?

TALTHYBIUS: Yes, Hecuba.

HECUBA: And all those words were leading in a roundabout way to one single word: 'killed'?

TALTHYBIUS: Yes, Hecuba. We cannot change facts;
We only have the words left to play with.

HECUBA: The words. A flood of words poured from my mouth –
in vain. My daughter has been killed.

Odysseus, I humiliated myself at your feet for nothing. And you looked
down from above at the spectacle of a mother's heart
shattering into pieces

and remained silent. What were my cries to you, entertainment

for the soldiers after the battle?!

When will you finally understand that your day too will come?!

ODYSSEUS: Your words, Hecuba, have shaken my heart. I
remained silent because in the face of a torrent

of words such as those I was struck dumb. Now you know.
And take some comfort,

if you can, in the following: Even if Polyxena were alive,

I would have been unable to alter her sentence. Therefore
don't torture yourself

with the thought that your pleas, had they arrived sooner,
might have helped.

I promise you: Nothing would have helped. Your
daughter's fate was death.

Also do not regret your tears of supplication, but turn
them into tears of grief,

and your kneeling turn into the prostration of mourning.

HECUBA: Polyxena is dead. Polyxena and death. How many times
will I have to mumble 'Priam is dead, Hector is dead,
Paris is dead',

until that coupling is stamped into my heart: Them and
their deaths.

And now Polyxena too. Polyxena is dead.

Go, Polyxena, join the row of corpses in my heart, rest in
peace.

But no: She rises, she walks, lives, breathes, laughs,

I lay her down – she rises, I cover her – she pokes out:

Go, rest now, Polyxena, lay down, I haven't the strength
to lay down more dead,

rest in peace, all of you rest in peace, be at peace and give
me some peace too.

Bring my daughter's body here.
I want to wash her and wrap her
in a shroud with my own hands.

TALTHYBIUS: Since we're not concerning ourselves here with
the sparing of sorrow,
and the tears have also already been shed, here, Hecuba,
put your tears
to further use, and hear the truth about your daughter's
death.
I'll just add in parentheses – I cried too.
And this is how the death occurred:

The entire army, rows upon rows, surrounded Achilles'
grave.
Polyxena was led there slowly by his son Neoptolemus,
a company of soldiers escorting her in order to hold her
during the execution.
When they reached the grave they stopped. The priest
lifted up a golden bowl
into which Polyxena's blood was to be drained after her
slaughter.
'Silence in the ranks!' I shouted, and the entire camp fell
silent.
Neoptolemus raised his eyes to the sky and prayed:
'Spirit of my dead father, drink the blood of the pure virgin,
princess of Troy, and be appeased, and let the wind fill
our ships' sails so that they may carry us home, to Greece.'

Thus he prayed, and the entire army whispered along
with him.
Then he drew his sword from its golden scabbard, raised
it in the air,

glinting in the sunlight, and motioned to the guards to hold Polyxena.

But she pre-empted him and said:

'Wait, Greeks. Let me die a free person. I am of royal blood, I will not run, I shall willingly present my throat to the knife: Just allow me to die free.'

'Free her!' shouted the army, and Agamemnon commanded the guards

to loosen their hold. And then with a proud royal gesture she gripped

the collar of her dress and tore it apart with such force

that the fabric ripped down to her waist, revealing to the sun

her white, beautiful breasts, gleaming with divine beauty in the light of the sunset.

Then she knelt down and said: 'Strike, I am ready!'

And for a moment longer there was silence, and then a muffled growl

arose among the soldiers, the sight of the pure white breasts against

the glimmering knife made them lose their minds, awoke in them

a dark and savage urge, and as one, as though a terrible storm were raging

through the camp, they attacked Polyxena,

hungry for woman's flesh, thirsty for blood, awash with a deep lust,

they grabbed her flesh, pulled her hair, dragging her, tearing her,

pouncing on her to squeeze and crush her, and without heeding their commanders' calls they ripped Polyxena's flesh to shreds,

and by the time the storm had subsided there was no
corpse left, but only
slivers of torn flesh, and scattered intestines, and the hands
of the soldiers,
still shaking from their frenzied passion, stained with
Polyxena's blood.

That is how your daughter's life on this earth came to an
end.

HECUBA: Were I asked yesterday what made a happy mother
I would have answered:
One whose children grow up, rich in good fortune and
possessions, happily married and producing rosy-cheeked
heirs. Were you to ask me today what made a happy
mother, I would say: One who gets to bury her children in
one piece.

Chapter Five: Andromache

ANDROMACHE: Polyxena is dead, and we have some
  issue with her death; And nevertheless – she is lucky,
  everything is behind her.

HECUBA: No, Andromache. Do not speak like that. You have
  a son.
  As long as you are alive, and even if your life is terrible,
  you have hope.

ANDROMACHE: I believe that being a corpse, is actually like
  having never been born at all.
  Consider the blessing in that: The dead feel nothing,
  not even the evil which befell them. If they could laugh,
  they would laugh
  whole-heartedly about the suffering over which they spilt
  tears while they lived,
  but they are also beyond laughter itself, so perfect is
  their rest.

  Polyxena is dead. And it's as though she never saw the
  light of the day
  on which her life was extinguished. Troy, her family, her
  life, her name –
  all foreign and distant, as though they never had anything
  to do with her.
  And so she rests, rid of the world and its obligations; and
  like all the dead,
  also rid of the greatest fear of them all: the fear of death.

  I, who lives, remember with every passing moment the
  happiness

I had and which was taken from me, and my name and
my fate sting me like a burn:
Andromache, widow of Hector, cursed slave.

Hector, to me, you were everything a woman's heart
could aspire to.
I came to you a virgin, I gave you all my soul and all my
strength,
the gods are my witnesses, I have no more in me; now,
emptied out, I must
cross the sea, to serve as a slave in the bed of Neoptolemus
son of Achilles,
how can I? How should I live this life from now on? And
with my new master's body lying on top of mine, and with
his thighs slapping against mine, what should
I feel? Should I betray the one and only true love I have
ever had? Or should I shut my eyes tightly,
and let the hate and bitterness shrivel my face, become
hated, beaten?
See my son Astyanax kicked around like a slave by my
mistress' sons?

You lament: 'Polyxena is dead!', and I –
have a different lamentation: Andromache is alive!

HECUBA: Andromache, beloved child, wife of my beloved
dead son,
I, Hector's bereaved mother, tell you with a breaking heart:
For Hector's sake – forget Hector.

Hector never existed. Your previous life never existed.
Look ahead,
obey your new master, yes, win over his heart, smile at him,
even if it is forced. This will benefit you and those who
accompany you. Think of your son, do this for him, I am
an old woman, my life is over, but you are

still young and beautiful, and your son Astyanax is a child,
all his milk teeth are still in his mouth,

and from the lowest rung on which we now are, the wheel
of fortune can

only turn in our favour, and turn it will, Andromache,
believe it! Believe it!

Open the gates of the world before Astyanax, and
perhaps, when he grows up, he will restore – after all he's
the only one left who can do so! – the glory of Troy!

Chapter Six: Astyanax

TALTHYBIUS: Do not hate me, Andromache. As you will have come to appreciate,
I myself do not decide anything. I am only a messenger.

ANDROMACHE: The harshest blows we have been dealt started with your soft reconciliatory words, Talthybius.

TALTHYBIUS: There's something in that. There is another piece of news,
and it is the most terrible of all for you.

ANDROMACHE: I am ready to die.

TALTHYBIUS: It is about your son.

ANDROMACHE: Are you going to separate us? Will you send him to serve a different master?

TALTHYBIUS: No one will make your son a slave.

ANDROMACHE: Will he remain here alone among the ruins of Troy?

TALTHYBIUS: Beneath the ruins.

ANDROMACHE: In prison?

TALTHYBIUS: Grave.

ANDROMACHE: My child!

TALTHYBIUS: To be executed. There, now you know.

ANDROMACHE: Astyanax will be executed?! A five-year-old child?!

TALTHYBIUS: That is what our army's war council has decreed. Hector's seed

cannot be allowed to live. The royal house of Troy will be
annihilated.

Accordingly your son Astyanax will be thrown from the
battlements of Troy

down to the abyss – to die.

Now give us your son, we will kill him. Accept
the sentence, be wise: you are a mother, yours is a
mother's heart,

but in the world there are not only mothers.

Do not hold your son tightly. Do not lie to yourself that it
is within your power

to prevent the inevitable. You have no one in the entire
world

to support you: You are lost, you are holding a dead child.

And if you are embarrassed to hand him over without a
struggle – consider this:

You are not a barbaric woman, you are a princess: no one
will condemn you with your stature – on the contrary – if
you detach from him simply like this,

with befitting dignity, bowing your head and accepting
fate.

And another thing: Do not insult our soldiers. You have
seen the army –

how hot-tempered it is. If you curse them, your child will
not be buried.

If you are quiet and peacefully accept that which awaits
you,

your boy's corpse will receive a funeral ceremony and a
burial.

And perhaps also you yourself, in light of your awful
tragedy,

will from this point on find the Greeks behaving more
softly towards you.

ANDROMACHE: Astyanax my infant son, they're already
talking about you like you're a corpse.
Astyanax – a corpse! Beloved child, a treasure too
precious to exist
in this loathsome world, your father's greatness is your
death sentence;
My wedding bells were also your funeral chimes.
Are you also crying now? Are you also able to grasp
what is about to be done to you? Your fingers are tightly
gripping
my dress, and I do not have the power to save you; you
have been sentenced to climb to the top
of the battlements, where you will shed your little life
like one removes a coat from one's back, and fall naked to
your death.

ASTYANAX: Mother, don't let them take me away! Don't let them
throw me from the battlements! What have I done,
I haven't broken anything! I played quietly in the
courtyard! Don't let them take me away!

HECUBA: Listen to this child! You're afraid of him?! A
shattered mother
and an infant child, refugees of a demolished city – are
they a threat to Greece?!

Listen to him! What does he want?! – to play in the
courtyard! Babies
are born poor; a sip of milk, a sweet, a cheap toy – and see
how happy they are! We are all still babies deep inside!
Search for the baby which is within you! Listen to that
child!

AGAMEMNON: I too had a little girl, her name was Iphigenia.

ANDROMACHE: Where is your wheel of fortune now,
Hecuba? In who's favour

will it turn now?! Where are the gates of the world
opening up before Astyanax,

where is the glory of Troy which he will reinstate, and his
milk teeth, Hecuba, when will they be replaced?!

HECUBA: I won't let you take him! I won't let you!
Cut off my hand, I won't let you!

ASTYANAX: Mother, don't let them take me away! Mother,
mother!

ANDROMACHE: Astyanax my son! My son! My child!
Astyanax!

HECUBA: Cries like these from a mother and her son will
rupture the heavens!...

Have they not ruptured yet? Still?! At least your hands
gripping the baby should have frozen!...

Have your hands not frozen yet?! Are they still gripping?!
But your heart,

it must have felt, just this once, a flutter of compassion run
through it!

Compassion, compassion, a flutter of compassion, it must
have, it must have...

ANDROMACHE: Give us another moment to say farewell. I
will not see him anymore.

Just one look, one final picture to bury in my heart.

Beloved child, one last, strongest hug, a warm living body,
the joy of my life! The smell of your body is so sweet! In
vain, in vain

I endured the pains of labour, in vain I breastfed and
dressed you in
white nappies and stood watch over your cot at night, it
was all in vain!...
Ahh, the wonderful taste of your touch, I'll never have
enough of it;

If I had known in advance how short our days together
would be –
I would have started this farewell on the day you were
born.

Greeks, barbarians, fathers of crime and cruelty, who
amongst you
would dare to shatter a life like this on the rocks below the
city wall?!

Helen, you were not created in God's image, but in the
image of cursedness and hatred;
the beauty of your face has killed my son, the beauty of
your face will cause my son's broken face to be covered
in blood; the beauty of your face has brought terrible
ugliness to the world!

Take him, you savages, lock him up, dump him,
kill him, end it, end it, and take me too;
my new matrimonial bed stands firmly on the backs of
coffins!

TALTHYBIUS: Come, child. The farewell rituals are over. Your
mother is already grieving over you.
Try to see it this way: evening has fallen. It is dark.
Time to sleep. Soon – you'll fall asleep.

There are those more eager than me to carry out such
assignments;
I was born to do what I am tasked with.

(TALTHYBIUS and the SOLDIERS exit with ASTYANAX. The PRISONERS sing to the child who's getting further away.)

PRISONERS: Your day is over, child, and so is the world,
    night has come and marches on,
    you had a ball to play with but
    it has dropped out of your hands, and gone.

    The world we lost will return in a dream,
    like an old, forgotten toy;
    close your eyes, rest your head on my lap,
    we'll say good night and sleep, sweet boy.

    Your life, dear child, was sweet,
    but the dream is sweeter still,
    and what was promised at dawn –
    in our sleep will be fulfilled.

    The world we lost will return in a dream,
    like an old, forgotten toy;
    close your eyes, rest your head on my lap,
    we'll say good night and sleep, sweet boy.

(TALTHYBIUS and the SOLDIERS return with ASTYANAX's corpse.)

TALTHYBIUS: On our way back we stopped by a stream, we washed
    the little body, we wiped away the blood stains.
    There, we spared you a heartbreaking task. Now
    you only need to wrap him up. Please,
    do it quickly, time is short,
    and the sails of our ships are already set.

HECUBA: Little head, covered in curls, a blossoming garden
    in which your mother and I planted countless kisses each
    morning;
    You once promised me, with your lips against my cheek:

'Grandma, when you die I will cut a lock of my hair, and place it on your grave as a sign that I will remember you forever.'
You broke your promise, my child, and it is I who is lowering you into
your grave, and I who will be remembering you.
And I will also remember this: Those remembering will themselves be forgotten too.

There was no place for him in the world. In a world where parents bury their sons, there was no place for him.

Chapter Seven: Helen

HECUBA: Kill her! Kill the monster already!
　　Blood-soaked nakedness, see the river of blood which
　　has already flowed from between her legs, and the blood's
　　still dripping!
　　Kill the monster already!

TALTHYBIUS: Yes, Hecuba, if you're able to take comfort in
　　this: –
　　We've come to the crowning glory of this tortuous
　　spectacle of the Greek war with Troy.
　　For ten years Greek soldiers have fallen because of Helen;
　　Troy itself
　　has fallen because of Helen; now it is Helen's turn to fall.

PRISONERS: Helen's blood! Helen's blood! Spill Helen's
　　blood!
　　How wonderful our lives – Helen's blood! Helen's blood!
　　What does a person even need besides a piece of bread, a
　　cup of water,
　　and a small trickle of blood from Helen's neck?!

MENELAUS: I am Menelaus, king of Sparta. My wife is the
　　most beautiful woman on earth,
　　and this is the happiest day of my life: today I become a
　　widower.
　　The man, Paris, who came to my home as a guest and seduced
　　my wife and ran away with her, has already paid the price.
　　He is dead. His country has been reduced to rubble.
　　And the woman, my wife, the one whose name I am too
　　ashamed
　　to utter, stands before me, my bounty from the war.

The army has handed her over to me to do with her as I please:
To kill her, if I wish, or take her to back to Sparta as a prisoner.

HECUBA: Kill her now, Menelaus, do not wait. Kill her before her gaze melts your heart.

MENELAUS: The days of melted hearts are past and gone.

HECUBA: Don't take her as a prisoner, Menelaus,
For it is her who will take you hostage!

MENELAUS: Silence, Hecuba! I already said I was going to kill her now!

HELEN: If so, Menelaus, why the big opening?
To scare me? We have not seen each other for ten years, for ten years
you've heard my words through intermediaries and messengers, some
distort them unintentionally, some distort maliciously, are you not curious for once,
even if it is the last time, to hear them from my own mouth?

HECUBA: Do not let her speak, Menelaus!

HELEN: Since when do you, king of Sparta, allow this old woman, this slave,
mother to your sworn enemy, hater of Greeks, to issue you with orders:
Kill! Don't take! Don't allow to speak!

I used to love you, Menelaus, and I love you today;
whoever wants to laugh can laugh, but deep inside you know it is true.

I have committed a sin of the flesh. Yes, the flesh is weak,
and my flesh is not

superior to yours, the men's, but Helen isn't only flesh,
and with her body

in Paris' embrace Helen remained yours. For the flesh I
get on my knees and beg

for forgiveness: for my soul I stand before you tall and
clean.

She calls me a monster, the old monster. She wants blood.
Notice how frugal she is with the blood of her sons, and
how much of a spendthrift

with the blood of your wife. I spent ten years in her
presence. I grew to

know the snake well. There is no love which she hasn't
poisoned; now, with

the final convulsions of her life,

she'll spit the last of her venom at the love of Menelaus
and Helen.

She calls me the destroyer of Troy; but has my own life
not been destroyed

together with Troy? Was I not a plaything

in your hands, men? My face is beautiful, did I create it?
I was but a mirror for you, projecting all the beauty and
the power

which you conferred on me; you, the men, control us,
and we, the women, are slaves; is it not a blatant injustice
for you to present us

as masters of your destiny when you are looking for a
scapegoat?

HECUBA: She talks about flesh, 'the flesh desired, the flesh
sinned', as though

she and her flesh were two separate creatures. In that case,
Helen, why

are you trembling so much for your flesh as its end approaches?!

With Paris you called your lust 'love', here, with Menelaus, you call your love 'lust'; and I am telling you, you whore, that you and your flesh, your soul and your love – are one filthy mush!

And this is how it happened, and I will repeat it untilI lose my voice:
My son Paris was an attractive young man; your heart, the heart of an adulteress,
was captivated by him. My son Paris wore golden tunics; your heart
was also captivated by gold. Your husband Menelaus had a modest palace;
In Troy, so you heard, the halls were grander;
And so, farewell, Menelaus – welcome, Paris!

In the war itself, whenever the scales tipped in Greece's favour, you suddenly remembered
Menelaus fondly; and when Troy had the upper hand, you forgot Menelaus,
and fawned over Paris. You followed the events, you watched the fortunes, not bound by anything, not by duty, not by emotion, not by loyalty or integrity,
just somehow always, always bound to luck.

You were with us for ten years, did you try to escape? And if you loved
your husband so much, and felt trapped in Troy, did you try
to put an end to your life? Did anyone ever find you tightening
a rope around your neck or pressing a spear to your chest?

No, Helen, your chest and your neck knew nothing but
ointments. Because the truth is
that you could have left. When I was queen, I beseeched
you to leave Troy.
'Go', I told you, 'my son will find another woman to love,
go, I will help you reach the Greek ships and put an end,
for them as well as for us, to this godforsaken war.'
The offer didn't appeal to you. Troy appealed to you,
Greece also appealed to you.
You enjoyed seeing the whole world losing its mind over
Helen.

Now without a shred of shame you dare to sit here, still
in your royal robes, sitting upright and watching, like
some spectator in the gallery,
the tragedies befalling others. Where is your heart? The
land is full of weeping women,
where are your tears? Where are the sackcloth and the
ashes on your head, where are your knees
to get down on, to crawl, to beg, trembling, for your life?
Everyone who has a mouth is shouting, and only you stay
silent?!

Oh Menelaus, these are my final words to you: you were
a man
in the battles, show yourself worthy of sealing your victory
as a man;
as you wipe out some spit in the sand with your heel, wipe
out the whore!

MENELAUS: Hold her hair, I'll slit this neck!

HELEN: You'll never have another neck like this, Menelaus!

MENELAUS: I never will, I never will! What a shame that
a neck like this belongs to a heart like this!

HELEN: Kiss it farewell. The world will see:
   There used to be love here.

MENELAUS: It's not you I am kissing, but my memories.

HELEN: You'll have nothing but memories left.

MENELAUS: There will be others, Helen.

HELEN: There will be others, but there won't be Helen.

MENELAUS: And have another kiss from this too!

(Passes the blade of his knife across her neck.)

HELEN: Blood! He has murdered me! Murdered!

MENELAUS: Not yet! She's shouting, which means: she's
   alive!

HECUBA: One more slash! Deeper!
   Go deeper, Menelaus, with the knife!

MENELAUS: Go deeper, hand!

HELEN: Not with the knife! Strangle! With your own hands!
   Let my neck feel
   the touch of your hands with my final breath!

(MENELAUS tosses the knife aside, grips her neck.)

Like that. Yes. Like a hug. Death by hugging. How gentle
your hands are.
Drops of my blood are seeping through your fingers, my
love,
as though you were removing red earrings from my ears
before bed.

(MENELAUS takes his hands off her neck.)

Take me with you as a slave. If you ever change your
mind and forgive me,

it won't be too late.

If you kill me now – there is no way back.

MENELAUS: There is already no way back.

HELEN: At least you will be able to use my flesh. After all you desire this flesh, and why would you deprive yourself of a great carnal pleasure which has come to you with the spoils of war?

MENELAUS: Yes, there is definitely material for the bed here.

HECUBA: It is lost! He will not kill her!

MENELAUS: During the day you will live in the pigsty.

HELEN: Or beside you in the palace.

MENELAUS: Never.

HELEN: And you want me to believe that Menelaus held Troy under siege

for ten years just for a slave like any other? Who is Menelaus,

a naïve thirteen-year-old boy who has never seen a woman's dress in his life?!

MENELAUS: Excuses upon excuses! Do you have any more? Bring excuses,

extinguish the fire of my torment with a flood of excuses!

HELEN: And what is it that has nourished you for ten years? Anger? Anger lives

for two days, a month; it was the longing, my love, which gnawed away at you for so long!

MENELAUS: I once loved a woman, she was so much like you.

HELEN: Menelaus, a strong man is not afraid to forgive. And
do not fear
what the others will say. Their concern is not for you,
but for their own entertainment, they want blood,
afterwards they'll pat you on the back,
'Indeed, you acted honourably, honourably'. And they'll
go home,
leaving the two of you alone in the room: you and your
honour.

Helen is yours, if you just take her.

MENELAUS: I am so tired.

HELEN: Come to me.

MENELAUS: A victory like this, only to say: I surrender!

HELEN: My scorned child. I embarrassed and I will console.

I always knew that our story was not yet finished;
Paris, all the others, were supporting characters, shadows
in the background,
in a play whose two leads are still active and illuminated.

MENELAUS: Brothers, I am taking her with me to Greece. I
think
she has learnt her lesson. People change with time,
mature, sober up, who among us has never made a
mistake and corrected it.

Brothers, I am taking her with me to Greece. For ten years
my wife Helen has been held captive by the enemy and
has waited for me,
now we are returning home, to our old matrimonial bed.

Brothers, I have tried to act honourably; but it is not
satisfying, honour.

Our lives are so short – do not condemn a man who
chooses to live.

(Held in HELEN's arms.)

Helen! Helen! Ten years in which my heart has been
weeping
under the armour! Ten years of toil to
extinguish a blazing fire which was more intense than me!

Chapter Eight: Hecuba

HECUBA: A moment ago you wanted to slit her throat, here's the knife!

MENELAUS: Huh?

HELEN: Menelaus, give her to me as a servant.

MENELAUS: She's already been given to Odysseus.

ODYSSEUS: Menelaus, take her.

HELEN: Servant! Bring me a towel to clean between my legs!

The circle has been closed, the end: Wiping the semen dripping
from the genitals of your children's murderer. From now until the end of your days
I will be an eternal knife forever twisting in your heart, a living testimony
to the mockery that fate has made of you.
Learn to say: Yes, madam Helen.

HECUBA: Yes, madam Helen.

HELEN: Learn to bow. Deeper. Bend over properly.
Learn to be a piece of furniture, just one of my various objects.

HECUBA: Indeed, fate…

HELEN: And also learn to shut up, to be mute. No more long speeches, no more emotional outpourings and bursts of tears.
A servant must serve: Emotions are meant for masters.

Hecuba, you are no longer the hero of this story. You've
been pushed aside.

From now on, in the story of my life, while I'm laughing
and dancing and treading,

you will be going in and out on your tiptoes, fetching a chair,
spreading a tablecloth in the unlit background of the stage.

HECUBA: Yes, madam Helen. I will be going in and out,
madam Helen.

HELEN: Show us. Serve us sweets.

HECUBA: Yes, madam Helen. Here, madam Helen.

HELEN: There will never be any more talking about yourself,
only

about the lives of the masters. Here, talk.

HECUBA: Madam Helen's skin is so smooth and sensitive
to mosquito bites, I'm very worried,

she mustn't sleep in the summer without a mosquito net...

TALTHYBIUS: Hecuba, would you like us to place something
on Priam's grave?

HECUBA: Priam?

TALTHYBIUS: Your dead husband.

HECUBA: Dead? I'm worried about Helen, we mustn't let the
mosquitos...

TALTHYBIUS: Because soon we'll all board the ships.

HECUBA: In that case, I must hurry and pack her dresses...

TALTHYBIUS: And also on the graves of your children,
Hector, Paris...

HECUBA: ...because if the dresses get wrinkled, how will she
be able to attend

the banquet which is taking place, so they say, on the deck this evening?

TALTHYBIUS: I am Talthybius, remember? I am the one who brought you all the terrible news.

HECUBA: Madam Helen is busy at the moment, she's not seeing any guests.

TALTHYBIUS: Hecuba…

HECUBA: Hecuba is dead.

TALTHYBIUS: Dead?

HECUBA: Didn't you know? Lying alongside Priam, Hector, Paris,
Polyxena, Astyanax and thousands upon thousands of others,
some above ground, some below, they're all surrounding her peacefully, and she is amongst them, wearing a silk dress, at peace.
That's how they're frozen, poised, as though at a ball,
a moment before the musicians are given their cue.

Talthybius, plant a tree on Hecuba's grave,
if you happen to pass by.

TALTHYBIUS: I am an old man. I don't happen to pass by places any more.

HECUBA: Remember her occasionally.

TALTHYBIUS: I will soon die, the memory will die with me.

Chapter Nine: The women

NEOPTOLEMUS: The great artist up above is calmly sketching the final lines
into the picture of war: You, the remaining women
and the virgins have been declared forfeit to the victorious army.
Woman by woman you will be taken by whomever takes you.

Women, women, the soft doughy paste, from which
we will knead the monsters of our heavy dreams.
It is as though there are two faces to him, to man: The first is the
smooth face of a baby, nestled against its mother's chest,
asking for milk, a sweet, a caress, as though its entire world depended
on a single drop of love. And the second, the face of a soldier returning from war,
charred, smeared with blood, pouncing on the woman, the fruit of his plunder,
tearing her flesh with terrible hatred and a hoarse growl,
as though trying to put out a blazing fire within himself
whose meaning he himself doesn't understand.

The fire has gone out, and now everything is ash.

END

THE LABOUR OF LIFE

Translated from the Hebrew by Naaman Tammuz

A comedy about a lifelong relationship approaching its painful end, with the husband striving to leave and his wife trying to keep him at home. 'You should see a psychologist', says the wife. 'What good will a psychologist do me?', asks the husband, 'He also wants to run away from his wife.'

Cast of Characters

YONAH POPOCH
LEVIVA, *his wife*
GUNKEL, *an acquaintance*

The entire plot takes place one winter's night in
our city, in the Popoch family bedroom.

Premiere	Habimah National Theatre, 1989
Director	Miki Gurevitsch
Costume and Stage Design	Ruth Dar
Lighting Design	Michael Lieberman
Music Composition	Yoni Rechter
Piano	Dani Donner

Cast:

YONAH	Nissim Azikri
LEVIVA	Lia Kenig
GUNKEL	Shimon Lev-Ari
THE CHILDREN	Gil Netanel / Lior Ravid

Act One

CHAPTER 1

Night. YONAH and LEVIVA are in bed. LEVIVA is asleep, YONAH's awake.

YONAH: I am a lost man. That's the inescapable truth: I am lost.

How did it happen that I was once a child, and the entire world
was laid out before me, and how did everything dissolve
and slip through my fingers? – these are all
worn out questions with worn out answers.

Only my pain isn't worn out in the least.
It's alive, it's fresh, it's right here. If only I could say,
'My dear heartache, crazier things have been known to
happen, people have lived and died, and all of them
have missed out in one way or another. It wasn't me who
invented disappointment or despair,
so would you be so kind, dear heartache, and subside,
subside – '
No, no, the pain – it hurts. When I'm in pain…it's like
I'm the first person on earth to have been hurt,
as though I alone in the whole universe were shouting:
'Yonah Popoch's life has come and gone,
gone is Yonah Popoch's life…!'

(He starts crying, suppresses his tears immediately.)

No, not like this Yonah. Get up
and do something, rescue yourself,
just don't lie here like a corpse.

(He sits up and gets out of bed.)

Here, be sensible: first step – getting up,

getting out of bed and cleaning it, shaking everything.
Lots of carcasses have piled up on this bed,
thirty years of rubbish.

(He looks over at LEVIVA, chuckles.)

She's sleeping as though nothing's going on,
snoring lightly, regularly, most likely dreaming
about some nonsense – this idiocy,
lying together in a double bed, mouths facing each other,
one sobbing, bleeding, the other
skiing down the Alps with a grin on her face, and this
is what they call married life, it's clearly all
a lie, a lie, so first things first,
let's clear this lie off the bed.

(He cranes over LEVIVA.)

What do I have in common with this piece of meat,
squeaking here in peaceful slumber,
gazing out at distant landscapes
in a dream from which I'm surely absent?

What do I have in common with Leviva? How did Leviva
end up in my life? Who arranged it that while I was still a
little boy, trailing along down the street behind my father,
some unknown woman would already be waiting for me
at some junction in my future, a woman with whom I
share nothing and who shares nothing with me, and that
some invisible glue, unseen but stronger than both of us,
would bind us to each other forever?

(He walks around the bed, not taking his eyes off LEVIVA.)

The birds arrive in the spring, fly away in the autumn,
tourists come for a month and leave, epidemics
break out, pass, everything moves and changes

and only one thing in the world remains fixed: Leviva.
And of all places here, with me.

(Lowers his head to LEVIVA's ear, whispers.)

What are we dreaming about, Leviva? Hiking in Switzerland?
A spot of skiing in the Alps,
while your husband's awake, listening to the water
dripping slowly into a leaky toilet somewhere in Asia??

Careful up there on the mountaintop, Leviva.
Ever heard of avalanches?
Here's an avalanche!

(He flips over the bed; LEVIVA drops out, hits the floor with a thud, lets out a yelp and gets up, startled, to her feet.)

Well, what? Pouncing already? Ready for a fight in the
middle of the night?
Who were you hugging up there in the Alps?

LEVIVA: When?

YONAH: Just now, in your dream.

LEVIVA: I never left the country.

YONAH: Liar! Prove it! Where were you hiding?
Who were you copulating with?

LEVIVA: I just went down to the street to buy a hat for the
summer.

YONAH: At night?

LEVIVA: In the dream it was morning.

YONAH: Very shrewd! Every allegation – you've got an answer!
And who was waiting for you in the hat shop?

LEVIVA: The shop owner.

YONAH: Did you copulate with or without hats on?

LEVIVA: I asked for a hat! There was only a hat there,
nothing more than the desire for a summer hat,
down in the street, in the morning. See,
even in my dream I didn't stray far from home.

YONAH: Oh God, what a cow, what a cow!
For the same price you could have dreamt about Switzerland!

LEVIVA: You never let me to dream about Switzerland.

YONAH: God, what a dumb animal! Even in her dreams
she won't let herself off the leash, God, what a
dumb corpse of an animal I've been given! And I've been
dragging this rotten cut of meat around on a leash for
thirty years now!

Doesn't matter, I'll soon be dead!
You'll end up a lonely bitch, wailing in the night with
no one for company,with no livelihood, then an armed
robber will break in in the middle of the night,
you'll scream 'Yonah, Yonah!' – there's no Yonah,
Yonah's resting alone in his grave, hands across his
stomach, in the dark, as though he was sitting in front of a
broken TV, waiting for the messiah as though He were a TV
repair man.

(Suddenly, the full weight of what's taken place dawns on LEVIVA.)

LEVIVA: I got thrown out of bed! I got thrown out of bed!
The man who stood with me under the chuppah, gentle
and blushing,
answering 'yes, yes' in a voice choking with shyness to all
the rabbi's proclamations, just threw me out of the bed like
you throw rubbish in the bin!

(She bursts into tears.)

What have I done to you? In my life with you, all I have
left is sleep.
I've never disturbed you or demanded anything from you.
I've wrapped myself up in my dream like a cocoon;
what have I done for you to rob me of even my hat in a
dream?!

YONAH: Now she's crying. Trying to melt me
with tears. Courage, Yonah!
In any worthy man's arteries there's
a drop of true Tatar blood!

(He sings her a serenade.)

You're crying, and gone are the years,
When your weeping would tear me apart,
Nothing, my dear, but your death,
Will melt the ice in my heart.

And a night breeze in the curtain,
Like a white sail on a windy day,
And my shoes, like a pair of anchored ships,
Call to me: get up, sail away!

You cry and I observe you
As one would a fly's convulsion,
Tearing off your wings in boredom,
With no gladness or revulsion.

And a night breeze in the curtain,
Like a white sail on a windy day,
And my shoes, like a pair of anchored ships,
Call to me: get up, sail away!

(Suddenly he starts hopping around her, like a man possessed, crying out rhythmically.)

Never, never, never, we will never fall!
Che, Che, Che! Che Guevara!
Che, Che, Che! Che Guevara!

CHAPTER 2

LEVIVA: I hope you're old enough
to understand by yourself that the problem here isn't me.

YONAH: Not you?

LEVIVA: Not me. I'm the pretext.

YONAH: So who is the problem?

LEVIVA: You. And there's nowhere for you to run,
because anywhere you go you'll be
carrying yourself around with you.

YONAH: You don't say! That's some deep insight, eh?
A real revelation!

(To himself.) Now she's going to suggest I see a psychologist.

LEVIVA: And I also think you should see a psychologist.

YONAH: What good will a psychologist do me?
He also wants to run away from his wife.
Everyone wants to run away, Leviva,
and you – as you may or may not be aware –
were born to be run away from.

LEVIVA: You want to go?

YONAH: I don't want to go – I am going!
Peeling off these green pyjamas

and heading off to the Bahamas.

What, didn't you realize that I'm finally abandoning you
like a pair of tattered old shoes?
Didn't you realize that these words
were words of farewell?

(LEVIVA starts crying. YONAH, to himself.)

And now she'll ask: Why?

LEVIVA: But why? Why? Wait!
You don't leave your home just like that after thirty years
without a word of explanation. You at least owe me an
explanation. If I've been doomed to spend the rest of my
life alone, at least tell me, so I'm not tortured by doubt –
why? What have I done wrong?

YONAH: Dear Leviva, don't you see that my entire life with you
was effectively finished the very first night we met.
Yes, we said everything there was to say that night;
the thirty years that came after it were merely based
on the fear of getting up and leaving.

Now, after thirty years, I can finally dare
to tell you: Madam, I have no use for you,
but to abandon you to your sighing, and for you to die alone.

(To himself.)

Now she'll ask if there's anyone else.

LEVIVA: And you? Do you have another woman?

YONAH: *(Laughing contemptuously.)*
Another woman!
From shit to the shitter, as they say.

All my life, day and night, I battle with the woman's stench,

hanging over my head
and threatening my struggle for purity.

Who are you? A backside! A backside attached to my legs
like a ball and chain! A backside that has brought me down,
narrowed my horizons, crushed my soul!

Understand me – because a man must be understood,
a man's inner workings are complex! – you can't base your life
on a backside. And even if at first the blood is warm
and the backside is firm, what happens over the years
as the backside shrivels up? What's left if from the very
beginning this relationship
consisted of nothing but a backside, a backside, while all
the rest, the beauty, the spirituality – for which I truly
yearned – had nothing to do with you?

LEVIVA: Beauty? Spirituality? Why didn't you say so?
Why didn't you ever bother to share your thoughts with me?
All you ever spoke to me about was salt herring – 'Why
didn't you buy salt herring, why in a jar, why not from
the barrel, and what about the Matjes herring, and why is
it pickled, and why no onions, the salt herring isn't fatty
enough, the salt herring isn't fresh enough,
the salt herring is salty, isn't salty!'
Now you're suddenly going on about 'beauty and
spirituality'?

As a matter of fact, spirituality is also my cup of tea.
Did I spend those two years at community college for
nothing? Try me.
If that's what this is really all about – it's still not too late,
believe me. Beauty, art, thought, they're never lost.
Why don't we start now?

I'll take Art History courses. I'll learn pottery.

You want nature? – we'll get Natural Trust memberships.
We'll travel. Just say the word.

Give me a chance, I won't disappoint you. The kids have
grown up and left,

we have free time. Here, let's get season tickets to the
theatre tomorrow.

Oh, the theatre, my old love. By the way, what have you
heard about that new play by that Russian that's showing
now, 'Seven Sisters'?

YONAH: You're getting confused with the seven dwarves. It's
'Four Sisters'.

LEVIVA: Aren't you getting confused with 'Four Carpenters'?

YONAH: It's four, you cow! 'Four Sisters'!

LEVIVA: Four, Four! Oh, I am a cow, an animal! What kind
of life have I been living! Forgive me, Yonah! Forgive
me, my parents and teachers! I know I've been a cow
and that I've lived my life like a dumb animal. From
now on everything's going to change. You've opened my
eyes, Yonah. Thank you, thank you, the shock was well
deserved, now give me another chance.

YONAH: I will not. I already hate the fact that you're vulgar
and common, but I'll hate you even more with a veneer of
culture and art. Don't deny your true nature, Leviva. You
are essentially a rear end,

don't disguise yourself as a pure soul. Because you know
as well as I do:

No pottery course and no theatre season tickets
will bring back what was never there to begin with.

LEVIVA: But there's also been some good in our lives, hasn't
there?

YONAH: It was all a lie. I was living a lie.
What I wanted – I never got;

and what I have – I never wanted.

I was borne along by the current like a dead fish.

LEVIVA: Yonah, listen, let's live our lives like we have
up till now, what do we actually have to be ashamed of?
We were good people after all, we worked hard,
we had children, raised them, we never broke the law –
everything was kosher. If we didn't reach the top, then
so be it – there's room for people like us too.

YONAH: Who are we kidding, Leviva? Ourselves?
Even if we keep our mouths shut, I'll be reminded every
second:
Life is happening somewhere –
and I haven't been taking part in it.

LEVIVA: I don't care what happens somewhere else!
If my whole world were a puddle – then that puddle
is where I've invested my life! And who would dare tell
me I've been living a lie?
I've lived my life with integrity; I haven't been given any gifts,
not from you and not from anyone else. I have lived like
decent people live. I've worked long and hard. What
exactly was the lie,
and, tell me, where exactly is the truth?

(She cries.)

I've treated you decently, Yonah, I have always
been decent, and why do I deserve this now...?

YONAH: 'Decent'. Yes, you have been decent. I have also
been decent. Two decent people.

Yonah and Leviva Popoch – a decent family.
Take a look at where decency has gotten me.
And God is laughing. God, as it turns out,

loves gangster movies. And we were counting on decency.

LEVIVA: I don't understand anything, I just don't
understand...
First culture and art, now
you want us to go rob a bank?

YONAH: *(In a gangster accent.)* You're talkin' too much.
You wanted an explanation – I gave you one. Be it the
backside,
be it any other reason:
I wanted something – and I don't have it.
And if that isn't clear enough, then here:

(He opens his mouth and makes retching sounds.)

I look at you and want to throw up. You've been
lying in my stomach like a stinking, rotten fish. Behold...

(He again opens his mouth and makes retching noises.)

– the essence of my entire life with you.
Now I'm opening a door and stepping out into the fresh air.

*(LEVIVA sits herself helplessly on the upturned bed, YONAH, to
himself.)*

Now she'll threaten to kill herself.

LEVIVA: Yes, go. If that's what you want.

YONAH: *(To himself.)* My mistake. The suicide will come later.

LEVIVA: I've been degraded enough for one night, haven't I?
Even though I still haven't told you
everything there is to say about you:
An ageing man with his ageing privates, in a panic.
What will you find outside, and who exactly do you think
is out there waiting for you?

But what does that matter now. I won't be able to
keep you here by force, will I? I don't have any
magic tricks left. How long
can you keep reheating the same chicken soup for
someone?

There's a woman involved, that's obvious to me. Either
you already have one or you're itching to go looking.
There are loads of young women.
And I've grown old. For thirty years I've served you,
and now Leviva – go off and retire.

So many new women are born all the time
and shove me aside. The world renews itself,
fresh colours and laughter and noise, and who remembers
the old-timers?
The grave – that's fine. But all the bland years ahead of me
before the grave – how can I bear it?

(She sobs.)

I'll kill myself…

YONAH: *(To himself.)* The suicide's arrived.

LEVIVA: It's not that I love you all that much,
but what am I going to do without you? And the
neighbours. How will I ever show my face in the street
again? How will I bear the shame? I'll kill myself!
I tell you I'll kill myself!

YONAH: Making a scene after all, are we?

LEVIVA: *(Screaming hysterically.)* Yes I'm making a scene! A
hell of a scene!
For all the neighbours to hear, for the entire city to hear,
I don't care! My husband's leaving me!
I'm being left on my own! My hands and feet

are being cut off!

YONAH: You won't keep me here with self-pity.

LEVIVA: *(Opens the window and shouts outside.)*
I am an old, sick, weak woman! My name is Leviva!
I used to be young! There used to be children here, noise,
and there was something to live for! Now I've grown old!
But I am the same Leviva! Deep down
I'm the same Leviva! I'm six years old!
I won't put up with this silence! Call the mayor!
I don't want a new flat from him,
I want my husband Yonah to stay with me!
Yonah is mine! Thirty years of my life have been invested
in him!
I want my thirty years!
Call my mother and father! I'm six years old!
I'm a bit ragged on the outside, but
that's just the plaster! And stop having so many new girls!
They get older and grow breasts!
They take my breasts and my skin
and use them without paying me! The sun used to be
mine! The world used to wait for me! And I was decent!
I'll stand proudly on any stage, I'll appear in front of
the UN General Assembly: I was decent!
The civilized world will have my blood on its conscience!
My blood will stain the conscience of the civilized world!

(She shuts the window and returns to the room, looking suddenly aged.)

YONAH: See? No one's responding, no lights are coming on.
Spilled blood doesn't get the civilized world out from
under its covers any more.

(He lifts the upturned bed, walks over to LEVIVA who's trembling all over, and sits her on the bed with a sort of pity and disdain.)

Ah, you cow, you miserable animal, you came into the world for no reason, and you'll leave it for no reason,
and everything that came in between also – no reason.

CHAPTER 3

LEVIVA: Come, Yonah, let's sit down calmly for a minute, all this hysteria's
already behind us, come. Let's be practical:
Where are you going, and what are you going to do?

YONAH: I'll find a cheap hotel, I'll sit there
for two or three days and look for a cheap one-bed flat.

LEVIVA: And once you're sitting in the cheap one-bed flat,
you'll look for a cheap fridge, two-three chairs, a cheap
bed, and then you'll lie on the cheap bed, and then you'll
get up and go out to look for a cheap woman.
You're finishing your life on the cheap.

YONAH: That's the price of freedom, isn't it?

LEVIVA: Freedom from what? And for what? To dump
a fifty-two-year-old woman, and then after toiling
and humiliating yourself to find a forty-seven-year-old widow,
and then teaching her from scratch how you like
your coffee, and how long the egg should be boiled for?

YONAH: *(Contemptuously.)* 'The egg should be boiled' – that's
all she knows, the egg should be boiled!
Leviva, open your eyes – there's a world around you, life.

LEVIVA: Oh yeah? Life? Come, sit, tell me all about it.
What sort of life's waiting for you? Sit, sit,

don't worry, I won't keep you here by force,
tell me like you'd tell a friend. A mate of yours. Shall I
open a bottle of wine?

YONAH: *(To himself.)* Now she'll remember that we're out of
wine. She'll offer tea.

LEVIVA: I think we're out of wine.
I'll put the kettle on for a cup of tea.

YONAH: Don't bother. No wine and no tea.
We need to talk, to finish, and if possible – to do it
honestly:

You asked me what I'll do? I don't know.
I don't have anything calling me, I don't have
anything pushing me.
I'm unhappy with you, not because outside
is better. It's just that with you the mystery's been lost.
I can read you too well. It's boring.
I know at every moment what you're
going to say. It's boring, Leviva.
Don't be angry at me for being frank with you – I'm bored
to death.

And maybe there is nothing in life, maybe it's all just
variations.
But that's the whole point: we need variations, we need
diversity.

LEVIVA: First a woman with a beauty spot on her chin,
then with one under her nose.

YONAH: And then another with one on the chin and one
under the nose,
and that way, with a few beauty spots here and there,

141

whoops – we've gotten through life.

LEVIVA: That's definitely one approach, although it's a little
idiotic.

YONAH: And if I'm being completely honest,
why not tell you explicitly:
I haven't loved you for a long time.
In a nutshell: you've passed your sell-by date.

(Tears well up in LEVIVA's eyes again.)

I'm trying to be open, and you – you start crying straight
away.

LEVIVA: That's how us women are built. We're not
loved – we start crying.
A man must be understood, you said,
a man's workings are complex; what about the woman?
Who will understand me?

YONAH: To each his own, as they say, I won't be able
to help you. And maybe this thing won't do you any harm
either, maybe you'll meet a widowed estate agent from Los
Angeles and laugh at me long and hard from America.

(LEVIVA suddenly bares her chest at him.)

What are you doing?

LEVIVA: Something banal. I'm offering myself.
The desire's greater than the ability, they say.
It might not look like much, might be a bit cracked,
but there's an urge for a farewell party.
Come to bed, Yonah, a beautiful farewell from Leviva.

YONAH: Cover your chest, Leviva. A bed
holds no appeal for us any more.

LEVIVA: *(Kneels in front of him.)* One last embrace. Instead of
wine.

YONAH: I'll come and visit.

LEVIVA: No you won't. And I want
to be left with the taste of a final embrace.
You owe me a last farewell embrace.

YONAH: *(To himself.)* The truth is, there's something exciting
about these farewells.
The face of a humiliated woman, awash with tears –
gets your hose hard.

(He sits beside her on the bed, inspects her closely. To himself.)

More precisely, semi-hard.

(She moves against him, he slides his arm around her. To himself.)

What's hard, who's hard?

*(She lies down and pulls him onto her. He tries to work himself
up, doesn't manage.)*

Listen, Leviva, you told me you'd been decent,
let's stick with decency. It really has
always been your strong side.

(He tries to escape her clutches. She doesn't loosen her grip.)

Leviva…Leviva…Levivuchka…
Understand…be an understanding wife…
I'm not leaving you through any fault of your own, it's
nature. It was nature that sprung me onto you that first
evening, and it's nature that's freezing me on the final
night.

(He again tries to escape, this time more vigorously. She clings to him tightly, lifts his shirt-tails and scratches angrily at his back. He lets out a yelp of pain, strikes her twice across the face. She lets go of him, he gets up.)

LEVIVA: I hope you know how much
contempt I have for you. I hope you realize that
you have no existence without me. Even the little that you
have accomplished,
the flat, the life, the fridge – it's all me.
Everything you're throwing away so dismissively,
and without which you're absolutely nothing – it's all me,
I made it, I built it, me, me,
I built a hole for Yonah the mouse.

(She sits up and gets out of bed.)

Just look at that audience. All those eyes.

YONAH: Where?

LEVIVA: Up there, on the ceiling all around. All the souls
of your dearly departed relatives and your dearly departed
friends, all of them like
an audience of spectators in the stands, sitting and watching.
Didn't you know that the souls are floating above our
heads all the time,
waiting to catch us in some mishap
or humiliation and roll about laughing?
What do you think their heaven is if not that?
There, up on that lamp, even your old mother's soul,
Alte Popoch, may she rest in peace.

YONAH: Mummy…!

LEVIVA: What did you think? That a mother wouldn't come
to see a son's humiliation?

Everyone, everyone's come especially to see you in your
disgrace.

Well, Yonah, now tell us about yourself.
I'm a stupid cow, a backside,
and what are you? Tell us about your life, Yonah.
Did you have big dreams? Did you yearn
to change the face of humanity,
to be a scholar, an inventor, a great artist?
Didn't you at least dream of being a singer?
There are some people who accomplish that.
And what about being surrounded by beautiful women
in expensive evening dresses? Where are all the women,
Yonah?
I only see one Leviva in a dressing gown;
What is this, a joke? Of all the women in the world
you ended up with Leviva in a dressing gown?

Well, there you go, promises up to the sky – and look
at yourself: After all those promises – I got left with the
promiser.

YONAH: You think you'll hurt me – you're mistaken:
You want me to admit I've failed? – I've failed!
I was too good for this world.

LEVIVA: All the mediocre people complain for some reason
about kind-heartedness.

YONAH: Yes, kind-heartedness.

(He points at LEVIVA.)

Here's all the good my kind-heartedness has done me.
My mother even told me: 'You're gentle,
too gentle and pure for this world,

you'll get cheated left, right and centre.'
Now this Leviva-in-a-dressing-gown is accusing me
of only having a Leviva-in-a-dressing-gown.
My kind-heartedness has killed me.

LEVIVA: He'll make himself out to be kind, he'll make himself out to be gentle,
he'll turn his failure into an entire philosophy,
anything not to admit the bitter truth:
You were basic goods, made of cheap material.

YONAH: She thinks she's torturing me.
I was a person just like everyone else.

LEVIVA: That's it, just like everyone else. Nothing special.

YONAH: Yes.

LEVIVA: Yes special?

YONAH: Not special.

LEVIVA: Kind of grey, worn out, kind of Yonah Popoch.

YONAH: What do you know about Yonah Popoch?

LEVIVA: I know you like I know my own warts.

YONAH: I have within me the depths of a bottomless well.

LEVIVA: You have within you the depths of the bottom of a cup of tea.

(She laughs in his face.)

Yonah Popoch and 'depths'!

(She holds his face in her hands.)

So you wanted, eh? You wanted depths, heights, there are none!

There's nothing. Where's all the joy from when you were born? Where are all the expectations?

Where are your parents' beaming faces when they held you for the first time,

wrapped in a thousand layers, like a precious pearl?

Mummy and Daddy are lying in their graves, and their beaming faces

are now full of despair, and the pearl was just a fake

made from a cheap material, from Popoch – have you ever heard of a material

called Popoch? – extremely common, a kind of sand, a soil, kind of like mud, you step on it everywhere,

sticks to the soles of your shoes: Popoch, popoch.

YONAH: *(Tears in his eyes.)* Terrifying. Terrifying. Kind of like mud. Soil.

(Suddenly he bursts into tears. He tries to talk through his tears.)

and what's…what's all the big…

what's the big…

I once saw our baby sleeping,

he was huddled in the corner of the bed, wrapped in a nappy and a blanket

like a little cocoon, so I told myself:

Who knows what he's dreaming about,

and he's lying there, a little bundle wrapped up in a couple of rags,

as though he had already been prepared for tossing into the pit.

And so for the rest of his life, even if he conquers half the earth, at night, huddled in the corner, he'll stink in his rags, bundled up tight to fit – into the pit.

So what's all the big…what's the big…

LEVIVA: *(Holds his hand as his crying gradually subsides and pivots with him towards the ceiling.)* Good evening, dear souls, you have just witnessed

a performance in Leviva Popoch's theatre of shame
with her old rooster, Yonah.

Lots of feathers flying about, lots of cock-a-doodle-doo,
and for the finale – always the same finale – we go back
under the skirt, and the skirt descends around them like a
screen.

If you've enjoyed yourselves, tell the other souls
in the sky about us, we'll be performing again in the same
place, at the same time, every evening. Good night.

And a good night to you too, Alte Popoch, rest your soul,
Did you laugh a little? Did you enjoy yourself? Oh, really,
stop.

It's nice of you to come. All the best to you, you sour little
soul.

YONAH: *(Starts crying again.)* Mummy...!

LEVIVA: *(At the ceiling.)* Ksssss! Go home! To the sky!

(To YONAH.)

There's no Mummy, Mummy's flown off to tell everyone
in heaven, tomorrow Leviva's telling everyone here on
Earth. That's how we've divided up the universe between
the two of us.

(She gathers YONAH up in her arms, rocks him side-to-side and sings.)

And when we first felt each other up,
I already knew in my heart of hearts:
simple merchandise made from dead-cheap parts.

We had no burning passion.
We chose each other, just like we were told.
Because rain falls in the world,
and because the nights are cold,
and because without a warm embrace
you can't make it through life at all.

But we could never rid ourselves of the smell of a market
stall.

(YONAH slowly leaves her arms. He is stooped and lifeless.)

YONAH: I feel unwell.

LEVIVA: *(To herself.)* The classic excuse for going back to bed.

YONAH: *(Stretches himself out on the bed.)* I feel very unwell.
Take me to Professor Bayer.

LEVIVA: To who?

YONAH: My mother used to tell me: when I was
a six-month-old baby I was very sick.
None of the doctors could help.
So they took me to the biggest expert.
That was old Professor Bayer.
Not 'Doctor' – 'Professor'.
He gave me a few drops of an unknown medicine
out of a small jar, and saved my life.

Now I need Professor Bayer.
I need another small jar with a few
drops of something the world has never seen,
and everything will be fine, and I'll start over.
Take me to Professor Bayer.

LEVIVA: Professor Bayer and his jar
  have probably been receiving patients in the sky for thirty
  years now. And until we join him up there I'm going back
  to finally buy that hat for the summer.

  *(She stretches out on the bed. YONAH struggles to get up, pale,
  breathing heavily.)*

YONAH: No, no, I'm not staying. It's now –
  or never. This is the grave. And I want
  the life that I've got left, I won't give up
  on the little that I have left, I won't give up…

  *(He walks on unsteady legs, gets dressed and packs a suitcase.
  LEVIVA sits up in bed stunned and wide-eyed, then shuts her eyes
  and sings quietly.)*

LEVIVA: We had no burning passion.
  We chose each other, just like we were told.
  Because rain falls in the world,
  and because the nights are cold,
  and because without a warm embrace,
  you can't make it through life at all.

  (YONAH lifts the suitcase and takes one step towards the door.)

END OF ACT ONE

Act Two

CHAPTER 4

LEVIVA is sitting on the bed as at the end of the previous act, her eyes shut. YONAH is standing, a suitcase in his hand, facing the door. A knock sounds from outside.

YONAH: Who's that knocking on the door at two in the morning?
Go see who it is.

(He goes back to the middle of the room. LEVIVA gets up, puts on her dressing gown and goes to open the door. YONAH shoves the suitcase under the bed and calls after her.)

Don't open until they answer you!

(LEVIVA comes back.)

Who is it?

(GUNKEL comes in after her, drenched to the bone.)

GUNKEL: Gunkel. It's Gunkel. Just Gunkel.
All in all nothing more than a Gunkel.
Why do I even bother saying Gunkel – barely a
Gunkerling.
And this is the thing: A trifling matter. A teensy-weensy
matter really. My head was hurting really badly. And I
didn't have any aspirin. And my head was exploding, and
the pharmacies are closed.
And I can't fall asleep. I went outside,
I said to myself: I'll pass by a friend's house.
And who is a friend? – Popoch. I passed by,
saw a light on and thought: If they're not sleeping,

I'll go in and ask about some aspirin. And maybe they
actually need some help? And I came in. Just for a
moment,
for an aspirin. A teensy-weensy aspirin – and I'm gone.
I wouldn't bother a married couple
at two in the morning with the lights on.
And by the way, what's with the lights being on?

LEVIVA: Would you like something cold to drink with the
aspirin?

GUNKEL: Why cold? It's night time, and December,
why not something warm?
Want me to drink quickly and leave?
I drink warm things quickly too.

(LEVIVA exits.)

And if I sit here for another five minutes,
what do you care? The lights were on anyway, weren't they?
Concerned for my time? Hee-hee,
don't be concerned, help yourselves, help yourselves.
There's more than enough.

(LEVIVA returns with a cup of water and a pill.)

Aah, cold after all.
Concerned for your time.
Want to get back to bed. If so
then the question remains: what's with the lights?

(Gestures towards YONAH.)

And why do you have your clothes on?

(He swallows the pill and drinks the water.)

Thank you. It's so nice here.

How lovely and pleasant, what an intimate warm life
is expressed and reflected in the folds of your bedsheets.
They must still be warm, the bedsheets, from the touch
of hot flesh. Were you in each other's arms? Were you
kissing?

(Touches the blanket.)

If so, why the lights?
And my head's still hurting.
My head, my head, my head,
Gunkel, Gunkel, Gunkel,
What do we do about Gunkel's head,
what do we do about the whole Gunkel?
Well, I won't keep you any longer,
the matters between him and her take precedence
over the matters between him and his Gunkelness,
hee-hee. Goodbye.

LEVIVA: Gunkel...

GUNKEL: Do I hear the start of an invitation
to sit and join the two of you for a cup of tea?

LEVIVA: You heard the start of me wishing you
a speedy recovery from your headache,
and a good night.

GUNKEL: Yonah, Yonah, why are you not saying anything?

YONAH: Gunkel...

GUNKEL: Do I hear the start of. . .

YONAH: Go home.

GUNKEL: Ah! explicit words, eh?
Sharp as a razor.

cutting into my brain,
but what do you care.
Gunkel's headache,
is inside Gunkel's head,
your head is clear, calm,
you just want to get back into bed,
but if you were already in bed
then why the lights?
And while we're on explicit words,
allow me to remind you,
that fifteen years ago,
also in the winter,
I loaned you a hat.
I want it back.

YONAH: I don't remember.

LEVIVA: Me neither.

GUNKEL: A brown cap, made of leather.
I want it back.

LEVIVA: We'll look in the cupboards tomorrow morning.

GUNKEL: I want it now.

YONAH: Have you gone mad? A hat search at two in the
morning? Go home, we'll find your hat – we'll let you
know.

GUNKEL: And you want me to sit at home like a mangy dog,
waiting for your messages?
I'll sit here, I'll drink a cup of tea and you'll look for it.
What were you doing up at two in the morning with the
lights on, anyway?

Weren't you looking for a hat? If not, then why the lights?

LEVIVA: The lights were on because they were on! Because
    my husband and I do it
    with the lights on! Because we have a rich and well-lit
    intimate life! Because we get far more aroused
    with the lights on! Because he gets to see in the light
    what you can only dream of seeing in the dead of night!

GUNKEL: I want my hat!
    I want my beloved hat right now!
    I'm not moving until I get my hat!

(He gets into the bed with his clothes on and gets under the covers.)

YONAH: Get out, or I'll throw you out – with the bed!

LEVIVA: Like rubbish gets thrown into the bin!
    My husband is a well-known overthrower of beds.

GUNKEL: I want a double bed so badly,
    I want a double bed so much!

LEVIVA: What difference does the size of the bed make?
    Whatever bed you get into – you'll still be alone.

GUNKEL: *(Squeaking like a mouse.)* Alone. Alone.

YONAH: Like a mouse.

LEVIVA: Yes, even his crying's not nice crying.

GUNKEL: I'm so afraid of dying alone.
    I was lying alone in bed,
    I couldn't sleep.
    Suddenly I was gripped with fear.
    My entire life was suddenly illuminated,
    and I saw it, all of it

from one end to the other, a narrow dark tunnel,
which I've been crawling through on all fours for fifty-five
years, lonely and frightened, and squeaking like a rat:
Gunkel! It's Gunkel! Just Gunkel!
All in all nothing more than a Gunkel! A Gunkerling!

(YONAH and LEVIVA cling to each other in horror as he speaks.)

Ah, what a happy couple.
two happy people,
coming together in front of my very eyes
in such an agonizing picture of happiness!

Popochs, you're hurting me
so very much. I am sick.
Take me to Professor Bayer.

LEVIVA: Professor Bayer for you too? Did he save you
as well with his little jar when you were six months old? God,
so that's what they've got going on in their heads, all of them,
under the big talk and the armour -
the desire to be carried in someone's arms
to see Professor Bayer? Tfu, babies!

GUNKEL: Take me to Professor Bayer!

YONAH: Professor Bayer's in the sky.

LEVIVA: With his jar. And if you're sick,
go and suffer in your own bed. Don't pass it on.
Go! Quick! You've sucked all the heat
out of our bedsheets. Hurry off to squeak
like a mouse back in your tunnel!

GUNKEL: *(Gets off the bed, looks at LEVIVA for a moment.)* Would
you allow me to touch you?

LEVIVA: I have a husband.

GUNKEL: Would you allow me to touch your wife for a
moment, Yonah?

YONAH: For what purpose?

GUNKEL: For the purpose of a small experience that will
serve me
for reminiscing in the night. May I?

YONAH: In which regions?
Not in the central frontal region,
and not in the central rear region.

GUNKEL: What do you call the central region?

YONAH: The hot and wild equatorial area
from the chin in the North to the ankle in the South.

GUNKEL: That's the equator? That's almost the entire globe!
You're leaving me with Alaska in the North
and Antarctica in the South. It's all frozen.

YONAH: Is anyone forcing you to go out on expeditions?
Stay at home, watch a slideshow.

GUNKEL: *(Gets on his knees.)* I'll just pop down to Antarctica
after all.

(Despondently kisses and strokes LEVIVA's feet.)

Yes, this is my life:
A visit to the freezing
frosty polar wastes,
licking a dry bone
which has been thrown to me like I was a dog.

(An embarrassed laugh escapes from LEVIVA's mouth.)

And mocking laughter, pouring down on me
from above, like saliva from the sky.

(He gets up, runs to the door, stops and turns to them.)

'Happy couple'! Tfu!
You think I don't know
why the lights were on.
Fighting like dogs in hell.
Sucking each other's blood.
'Happy couple'! We've heard all about you!
Forming a coalition in front of lonely people –
is the only thing you know.
A coalition of hate.
You can't fool me. Not
Gunkel. Gunkel knows a bit
about life. Gunkel's opened a book
or two, Gunkel knows about weddings,
families, beds, newborns. Gunkel
doesn't buy it. Gunkel spits
on it. Gunkel couldn't care less.
Even when Gunkel's crying about his own life -
Gunkel spits on the lives of others.

And I want that hat
which I loaned you fifteen years ago.
I'm not giving up that hat.
I'll come back tomorrow, I'll come back every night,
until you give me back my hat.
You didn't even offer me a cup of tea.
Just cold water.

(He suddenly bursts into tears.)

I know how bad you have it, but at least

you have each other to bark at.
I don't have anyone to bark at.
Alone, at the ceiling, in the night –
woof! woof woof ! woof !

(He exits.)

CHAPTER 5

YONAH is sitting on the bed and sobbing quietly.

LEVIVA: Why are you crying?

YONAH: Because there's no escape. Half an hour ago
    I wanted to leave. Now I know:
    There's nowhere to go. We're all Gunkels.

    There's a Gunkel with a wife, there's a Gunkel
    without a wife, but wherever you run to –
    we're all Gunkels.

LEVIVA: You're not a Gunkel.

YONAH: I am a Gunkel. Deep down
    I'm just a Gunkel. A Gunkelkin.

LEVIVA: No, you're not a Gunkel. You're a Popoch.

YONAH: What a bargain! Really! It's a brilliant choice
    life presents you with: you're either a Gunkel,
    or you're a Popoch. What a great bargain!

LEVIVA: You are Yonah Popoch and you have a Leviva
    Popoch.

YONAH: Another bargain!

LEVIVA: And a brief appearance by Gunkel in the middle of
    the night

suddenly breathes new life into the love that had withered
between Yonah and Leviva.

YONAH: There's no love here, just the fear
of being alone at night.

LEVIVA: I'm not going to argue with you about words.

YONAH: And even that's only for half an hour.

LEVIVA: A half hour and another half hour,
life is made up of lots of half hours.

YONAH: I wanted something more.

LEVIVA: Here's all of me. This is all I have in me.

YONAH: I hoped for something more.

LEVIVA: Well, there is nothing more.
We'll grow old together, Yonah; together we'll make it
all the way through life
without anything more.

YONAH: Yes, the book of life has basically been written
apart from a single empty line for the end date.
It's not an easy thought to get used to, but
I must get this into my head:
There will be nothing more.
Nothing more is going to happen.

First I ate chicken at my mother's,
then I ate chicken at my wife's,
I'll eat a few more portions of chicken in hospital,
and then – time to lie still, to rest –
once and for all without any chicken at all.
Those are the chronicles of Yonah Popoch.

(LEVIVA dances him around.)

What are you doing?

LEVIVA: The doctors recommend dancing.

YONAH: You say and do stupid things
    so naturally, like a fat cat yawning
    in the sunshine. And the worst thing is
    that your nonsense is actually correct:
    'The doctors recommend dancing',
    'Life is made up of lots of half hours' –
    it's all so true that's it's terrible.

(He starts crying again.)

I'm scared of dying, Leviva,
    I'm scared. Gunkel's going to die,
    and I'll die too.

I'll lie alone in the dark – a Gunkel.
    The dead all turn into Gunkels.
    Who will fill the green pyjamas
    that I'm going to leave behind?

LEVIVA: No one will fill them, Yonah.
    The green pyjamas will stay empty.
    And there's something else you have that Gunkel doesn't.

YONAH: What?

LEVIVA: If you die, I'll remember you.
    Here, look into my eyes, your image has been
    embedded within me for safekeeping. I'll remember you.

YONAH: Etch me in your memory, Leviva,
    because I'm scared of disappearing.

LEVIVA: I'm etching,
I'm etching every tiny detail.

YONAH: And wasn't I a bit of a faded character,
who disappeared without leaving a trace?

LEVIVA: God forbid. You've made your mark on the world.
You have marked.

YONAH: You can drop the wrinkles from the picture.

LEVIVA: The wrinkles don't bother me.

YONAH: You married a young man with a smooth face,
the wrinkles weren't part of your commitment.

LEVIVA: All of it, I got all of it, I committed to it all.
It was all mine, we were together, I'll remember it all.

Etch me in your memory, Yonah.

YONAH: You're already etched.

LEVIVA: Not just my bum.

YONAH: No no. Also the devoted, placid look in your eyes.
I won't forget you, Leviva.
You've touched my heart, you've touched the very bottom
of my heart,
you, your life, your nagging, your boundless
devotion. The hard labour with which you've worked
the failed endeavour of our life. How simply, Leviva,
you took your life, like someone takes their toothbrush,
and placed it in one glass with mine.
I won't forget you, Leviva.

(They bring their heads together, forehead to forehead, and look straight into each other's eyes, murmuring prolonged syllables like children....)

YONAH AND LEVIVA: yyyyeeeeeee…

YONAH: Here we are, exchanging final pictures,
    and burying them deep inside, as though
    preparing for a long separation, and maybe forever.

LEVIVA: And keep a warm place for me next to you beyond
    the grave, if you go before me.

YONAH: Oh Leviva, you and your errands
    all the time: should I also take the rubbish down
    with me when I go down to the grave?

(He lays her down on the bed, tries to have intercourse with her.)

LEVIVA: Come, Yonah, come…my love…
    So many nights I've been waiting for this…

(He doesn't succeed, she tries to help him.)

Come, Yonah…come…

YONAH: Shut up, shut up…

LEVIVA: Maybe you're tired.

YONAH: Shut up…

LEVIVA: If it's not happening, don't worry about it, leave it,
    get some sleep, relax, we'll pick up where we left off
    tomorrow…

YONAH: Shut up, I said…tomorrow, tomorrow, we're both
    getting older by the day…

LEVIVA: Sssshhhh, just don't start again,
    relax, I'll make a cup of tea…

YONAH: *(Gets off her.)*
    The eternal solution – a cup of tea!

Go drown yourself in your tea!
I don't need your pity,
save it for yourself!

What have I done? I haven't solved anything.
We've exchanged a couple of soppy-emotional words,
and again I find myself lying
in the same grave, with the same carcass.
That's their power, to melt and blur everything
in a porridge of tears and tea and pangs of conscience.

And I haven't solved the main problem: What to do
with what's left of this life? How to breath?
And in which bed to finally lay my sack of bones
to rest – Popoch's or Gunkel's? Or are there
other beds apart from those?

LEVIVA: You started off with culture and art – and ended up
with beds.

YONAH: And you, don't delude yourself: what droops here
with you – leaps outside like a young jaguar!

There's no shortage for me. There are
lonely women scattered around the world like rubbish...

LEVIVA: Go to them! To the rubbish!

YONAH: I will! I'll go! I wanted to go earlier,
but you started crying like a crocodile, and I
took pity on you, and what did I get out of it? I'm missing out!
Oh, the number of affairs that I've missed out on
because of my merciful heart!

LEVIVA: So go, go already! Who's stopping you?
Run quickly so you don't miss out, your suitcase is already
packed. Earlier I was begging you to stay, that's true, now

I'm telling you. Out! Off to the jungle with the jaguar!

YONAH: What, and give you the satisfaction and pleasure
of me going and you staying here?
Vacating the bed, the armchair,
giving up the flat, the TV,
the government bonds in the bank,
so that's what you're waiting for, is it?
No, no, I'm staying right here with you,
with you on the balcony, in the kitchen and in the bed
to make your life miserable.
I'll screw outside – and I'll fart at home!

We'll grow old together, and we'll rot together,
and together – linked to our
inflation-linked bonds, listed in both our names –
we'll go down to the grave!

Ring the bells, sound the sirens,
Summon the masses to the squares and the streets –
Yonah Popoch's life has gone!
Gone is Yonah Popoch's life!

LEVIVA: *(Laughing in desperation.)* Bells? Sirens? Tee-hee,
here's your tune. Hear that? –
the sound of water dripping into the toilet bowl;
it accompanied your life,
and it'll accompany your death as well.

CHAPTER 6

YONAH: Leviva, I feel very unwell.

LEVIVA: *(To herself.)* The jaguar retreats into its lair.

(YONAH sprawls out on the bed.)

What a surprise.

YONAH: I have a pain in my chest and I'm nauseous,
    I need to throw up.

LEVIVA: *(She watches him, the look on his face worries her.)* Let's
    go to the bathroom, you can throw up.

YONAH: The signs are worrying. I'm scared to get up.

LEVIVA: Nonsense. My money's on an upset stomach.

YONAH: I'm not in the mood for gambling.
    Promise me it's not a heart attack.

LEVIVA: What are you talking about, Yonah,
    you're a healthy man.

YONAH: Promise me it's not a heart attack.

LEVIVA: I promise.

YONAH: How do you know? Are you a doctor?

LEVIVA: I trust my instincts.

YONAH: Ah, your instincts, your words, your promises.

    (He sits up in bed.)

I'm reminded of my mother. On her deathbed
I promised her she wouldn't die.
She also trusted me. And now
I'll pay the price of that disappointment
which I bequeathed to my mother.
Each generation bequeaths despair to the next.

    (He collapses backwards. LEVIVA screams.)

LEVIVA: Yonah!!!

YONAH: Ssshh…why are you shouting? What are you doing?

Trying to distract me from the most important thing
that's about to happen to me, that you no longer have a
part in,
and no one else does either, only me alone,
this time for real, once and for all, finally alone?

LEVIVA: Yonah! I'm calling a doctor! Yonah!

YONAH: Ssshh – no, why? Feel better already. Big relief.
Something inside me has been disconnected, a stone has
been pulled out. It's like my life until now had been some
sort of small dirty laboratory
full of experiments. The time for experiments has now
passed, a door
has opened, now I'm standing on the threshold of life itself.

LEVIVA: And the chest pain?

YONAH: Gone. You guessed correctly, as usual. An upset
stomach.

LEVIVA: You worried me so much all of a sudden:
Your heart, in the middle of the night.

YONAH: Night? What night? Can't you see
that it's Saturday morning, and that I'm on the way
to the synagogue with my father?

Saturday morning. Look: A father walking
with his son to the synagogue.
Son and father hand in hand.

The father's walking and humming quietly to himself, the
son kicking little stones.
Each with his own preoccupations, in the empty street,

bathed in such tranquillity, in a light of grace.

Hand in hand, a father walks with his son
to the synagogue.

(He dies. LEVIVA screams.)

LEVIVA: Yonah, don't die! Don't leave me, Yonah!
We've still got to grow old together, have you forgotten?
All the hard, back-breaking labour, the labour of old age
and decay, the day-to-day work of despair,
the diseases, the fading strength, and the fear –
oh, the mortal fear crawling in the long sleepless nights –
It's not fair of you to leave it all on my shoulders,
I don't have the strength on my own.

Yonah, get up! The morning's approaching. The gate
to the old workshop of our lives is creaking open.
Get up for work, Yonah. Get up so we can go together and
finish the labour of life!

Epilogue

LEVIVA is sitting at deceased YONAH's bedside. Her voice is soft.

LEVIVA: What would it have mattered to you, Yonah, to live a
little longer,
we would have strolled arm in arm in the early evening,
you would have grumbled, I would have agreed,
who can be bothered to fight any more, old age
is a great remedy for married life,
how right it is for a husband and wife to grow old together.

(She sees herself and him as an elderly couple. They sing.)

LEVIVA: Will you remember a young boy's smile, a ray of
sun, a glowing ember?

YONAH: Yes, I'll remember – a glowing ember...

LEVIVA: The young boy's smile will not return, nor the ember
nor the sun,
nor the world in which we loved to be
it won't be back, it won't be back, it won't be back for us
to see.

(To an imaginary boy.)

LEVIVA: Will you remember us, little boy playing in the yard?

YONAH: Yes, remember us – there in the yard...

LEVIVA: We won't be back in the yard again, we won't be
back to see you play
we won't be back to walk together on this sodden lump
of clay we won't be back, we won't be back, we won't be
back again.

YONAH: *(Getting up laboriously from the bed, grumbling.)*

I've done very badly in life.
The stream of the leak in the dripping toilet has reached
its peak – The stream of the urine has become more weak.

LEVIVA: We didn't know back then that we'd become
such losers, eh?
Back then we thought we had it hard. We didn't know,
how much worse it could get.

YONAH: What?

LEVIVA: *(Shouting.)* We didn't know how much worse it could
get!

YONAH: I always knew.

LEVIVA: In any case we also had
some good moments.

YONAH: I can't hear.

LEVIVA: *(Shouts.)* In any case we also had
some good moments!

YONAH: Can't remember.

LEVIVA: We did, we did. A long time ago.

YONAH: There was nothing, old woman.
The flow of urine used to be at its peak –
now it's weak.
I've done very badly in life.

LEVIVA: And I would ask that someone write
a book about my life.

(To the audience.)

Excuse me, I may be a foolish woman.
Nevertheless: I've lived a little. I've been through something.

And if there's a writer sitting amongst you this evening,
and if he's in need of some interesting material,
I'd be prepared to meet him and tell him.
I won't ask for any payment, I wouldn't even care
if he made up some fake names. It's not the respect I'm after,
or the money, just a little understanding, and for some
small memory to be left behind after us, so that people
know: we lived.

YONAH: What?

LEVIVA: We lived!

YONAH: 'We lived'! Big deal! Our lives
are of no interest to them.

LEVIVA: Our lives must be of interest to them!
They were once their lives too.

(To the audience.) Here, I'll even tell you a juicy secret:
Twenty years ago my husband Yonah got up
in the middle of the night and wanted to leave me.

YONAH: What?

LEVIVA: I'm telling them about how you wanted to leave me!

YONAH: Really? Did I? There were a thousand times
I wanted to leave, so what?
Everybody wants to leave. Everyone.
Look, they're laughing, this is boring them.
Me wanting to leave is boring them.
My urinary tract is boring them.
Our entire lives are as boring as hell,
not just for us, but for the audience too.

LEVIVA: Still, our way was different.

(To the audience.) Dear Mr Writer, our way was our way.

YONAH: She's a cow, the old woman, what can you do –
always was. Ageing goes well
with brutishness – like cream and bananas.
I've done very badly in life.

LEVIVA: Writers and artists, cultured people, look at us!

YONAH: 'Go to hell', says the writer, 'you and your comical
lives!' – even though his life, the writer's
is no less ridiculous – 'You're holding mankind up!',
he says, 'we're on the threshold of a new age', –
they're always on the threshold of a new age – 'people are
flying', he says, 'to the moon, and you stick to the shoes like
mud, and keep churning the same rubbish again and again!'

LEVIVA: Not rubbish! Not rubbish!

YONAH: Only rubbish! Rubbish, rubbish and precisely
rubbish! And I specifically don't want them to write
anything! No pages, no memory!
Lives like these deserve to be erased as though they never
existed!

LEVIVA: No no! I can't believe it!
Arise a writer. A noble man, with a conscience,
with a soul and a heart. He'll understand. He'll listen and
understand.
He'll hear the entire story of our life, he'll find
the right words, he'll make something beautiful out of us,
something deep, full of compassion and emotion. Because
even with all the mistakes, the defects, there's enough
material left in us for a good piece.
Oh God, he'll understand us, he'll understand,
he'll understand, he'll understand, he'll understand!

YONAH: *(Calming her, walking her gently back to the bed.)*
   Ay, you cow, you cow, no one will understand, no one
   will write, there's nothing to write about, everyone's
   already yawning. Good night.

   *(He sprawls out on the bed, laying there as before, dead. LEVIVA sits
   near the head of the bed and sings to him, like a lullaby.)*

LEVIVA: We won't be back in the yard again, we won't be
   back to see you play we won't be back to walk together on
   this sodden lump of clay we won't be back, we won't be
   back, we won't be back again.

END

WALKERS IN THE DARK

A Nocturnal Vision

Translated from the Hebrew by Jessica Cohen
and Evan Fallenberg

This 'Nocturnal Vision' tells the stories of nameless characters, dead and living souls, wandering thoughts, a storyteller, and even God, as they roam on an overnight journey. Will they find what they are looking for? One of Levin's most existential plays, it depicts the essence of human experience on the stage.

Cast of Characters

THE INTANGIBLES:
THE NARRATOR
GOD

THE LIVING:
WALKING MAN
WAITING MAN
EVASIVE MAN
TRIVIAL MAN
SQUEEZING MAN:1
SQUEEZING MAN:2
SQUEEZING MAN:3
THE NEIGHBOR
EVASIVE MAN'S CANADIAN MOTHER

THE DYING:
MOTHER OF WALKING MAN
MOTHER OF WAITING MAN:

THE DEAD:
MOTHER OF TRIVIAL MAN
MOTHER OF EVASIVE MAN
MOTHER OF WALKING MAN'S MOTHER
FATHER OF WALKING MAN'S MOTHER
TIRED DEAD MAN
DILIGENT DEAD MAN
BITTER DEAD WOMAN
SHY DEAD MAN
GENTLE DEAD WOMAN

ANGRY DEAD MAN
VULGAR DEAD MAN
DESPAIRING DEAD MAN
DEAD TOT
SOUR DEAD WOMAN:

THE THOUGHTS:
VAGUE THOUGHT
MURKY THOUGHT
PICKLED HERRING THOUGHT
ASS THOUGHT
LAJAN THOUGHT
CHOCOLATE THOUGHT
TROUSER THOUGHT
PYRAMID THOUGHT
CHILD THOUGHT

Premiere	Habimah National Theatre, 1998
Director	Hanoch Levin
Costume and Stage Design	Rakefet Levi
Lighting Design	Shai Yehuda'ee
Music Composition	Yossi Ben-Nun
Musicians	Guri Agmon, Yossi Ben-Nun, Vered Ya'akov, Avner Yifat, Roni Holen

Cast:

THE NARRATOR	Dov Reizer
GOD	Avraham Mor
WALKING MAN	Yehuda Almagor
WAITING MAN	Michael Koresh
EVASIVE MAN	Dror Keren
TRIVIAL MAN	David Kigler
SQUEEZING MAN:1	Luis Rosenberg
SQUEEZING MAN:2	Eliezer Apelboim
SQUEEZING MAN:3	Robert Henig
THE NEIGHBOR	Alex Cohen
MOTHER OF WALKING MAN	Rosina Cambus
FATHER OF WAITING MAN	Alex Monte
MOTHER OF TRIVIAL MAN	T'khia Danon
EVASIVE MAN'S DEAD MOTHER	Tzvi Kanner
MOTHER OF WALKING MAN'S MOTHER	Myriam Nevo
FATHER OF WALKING MAN'S MOTHER	Lupo Berkovitch
TIRED DEAD MAN	Yitshak Levi
DILIGENT DEAD MAN	Dan Harden
BITTER DEAD WOMAN	Lia Dolitskaya
SHY DEAD MAN	Nahum Buchman
GENTLE DEAD WOMAN	Menora Zahav
ANGRY DEAD MAN	Giora Shamai
VULGAR DEAD MAN	Shmuel Shilo
DESPAIRING DEAD MAN	Mordechai Ben-Ze'ev
DEAD TOT	Yossi Segal
SOUR DEAD WOMAN	Rina Rosenbaum

EVASIVE MAN'S CANADIAN MOTHER   Avraham Plata
VAGUE THOUGHT   Assi Hanegbi
MURKY THOUGHT   Uri Avrahami
PICKLED HERRING THOUGHT   Ofer Zohar
ASS THOUGHT   Avraham Selecter
LAJAN THOUGHT   Tracy
Abramovitch
CHOCOLATE THOUGHT   Avraham Plata
TROUSER THOUGHT   Tzvi Kanner
PYRAMID THOUGHT   Alex Cohen
CHILD THOUGHT   Daniel Magon/
Noy Barak

Act One: Walking Man

I

WALKING MAN is sitting on a bed, at night. There is a suitcase at the foot of the bed. He stands up, lifts the suitcase, looks down at his feet, at the suitcase, at the sky, and then at his feet again.

WALKING MAN: *(To himself.)*

First there is this matter of standing on your feet and not falling. How strange that such a narrow bit of foot can serve as a base. And then there is the strange matter of a suitcase, a box with a handle that you put things in for the road. What road and what things – that's a question, but a separate one. Then there is the strange matter of night, and it's dark, and you can't see, and so you also don't know. And this combination of feet, suitcase, night – very strange. It's all so very strange, as though the things were once tied together but came apart. *(He takes a step.)* You swing one foot forward. The space between the two feet is called a step. You take a step. You are no longer in the place where you were standing, and in the place where you were not standing, now you are. Standing. And that's strange, too. Everything is shrouded in fog. Another step. Now it's actually walking. I am a man, and I took two steps, and now here I am, a walking man. A person who cannot sleep, who happens to be peering at me through the slats of a shuttered window, says to himself, 'Here is a man walking. I wonder where to.' Yes, someone is wondering about me briefly in the world.

Enter the aged MOTHER OF WALKING MAN, wheezing and out of breath.

NARRATOR: *(To the audience.)* The Walking Man does not
know that while he walks the streets with a suitcase, his
beloved mother lies alone two blocks away, critically ill
without anyone to pass a hand over her forehead.

WALKING MAN: *(To himself.)* I forgot to mention that while I
walk at night with a suitcase, two blocks away my beloved
mother is sleeping peacefully, dreaming sweet dreams,
feeling wonderful, no longer constipated. *(MOTHER OF
WALKING MAN exits.)*

III

Enter TRIVIAL MAN with a suitcase, dragging behind him his mother.

NARRATOR: *(To the audience.)* This man is a different man,
trivial, our story is not about him. He is just a passing
character here, unnecessary. At the same time he feels that
he is a man, too, and he has a suitcase, too, and he is at
night, too, the same night spread across the skies of our
land.

*(He gestures to TRIVIAL MAN to exit; TRIVIAL MAN points to his
dead mother.)*

(To audience.) I forgot to tell you that Trivial Man doesn't
even have a mother, she died long ago, he is alone in the
world, no one on earth for him to even watch die.

TRIVIAL MAN: Why did I go out? Sometimes a person wants
something, wants it so badly...!

(Exits with his mother.)

WALKING MAN: *(To himself.)* I will set out on a night journey
to visit my friend so-and-so. And if I am asked by myself
what's up with me, why am I not sleeping peacefully, why
get out of bed suddenly and walk the streets knocking
on doors in the dead of night, I will tell myself that I am
walking as part of a comprehensive plan that I cannot at
this time divulge to anyone. My friend so-and-so will think
me mysterious or at least a man not without purpose. *(He
walks.)*

Act Two: Waiting Man

|

WAITING MAN is sitting on a bed, in the dark, a suitcase at his side.
WALKING MAN knocks at his door.

WAITING MAN: Who's there? Are you finally here? After so
many years of anticipation…! I thought I would go crazy
missing you! Why did you make me wait?! I sit on my
bed, dressed, with the suitcase at my side, waiting for you
night after night! Why this torture, my love?

WALKING MAN: Hello.

WAITING MAN: Who is it?

WALKING MAN: So-and-so.

WAITING MAN: *(Letting him in, disappointed.)* Hello.

WALKING MAN: Dark.

WAITING MAN: Night.

WALKING MAN: Can't see.

WAITING MAN: Why did you come?

WALKING MAN: I'm paying you a short night visit for urgent
reasons, which you yourself understand I cannot divulge
to you at present. *(To himself.)* I am stirring a supreme
curiosity in him.

WAITING MAN: *(To himself.)* It is highly possible, even
probable, that he knows something about my departed
love and is planning a wide-scale surprise for me. I'm
clearly about to be dealt a big piece of happiness. *(To
WALKING MAN.)* Of course I've been waiting for you.

WALKING MAN: Were you sleeping?

WAITING MAN: Certainly.

WALKING MAN: In your pajamas?

WAITING MAN: Briefs.

WALKING MAN: And at your side a warm-bodied lover breathing steadily, her hair cascading over a snow-white pillow.

WAITING MAN: Naturally.

WALKING MAN: Life, the simple, peaceful life we all aspire to when evening falls. *(Grumbling.)* He doesn't ask if maybe I'm feeling pressure on the left side of my chest.

WAITING MAN: I understand you're feeling pressure on the left side of your chest.

WALKING MAN: I am. *(Again grumbling.)* He doesn't seem all that concerned.

WAITING MAN: I strongly suggest that you go first thing in the morning for a full checkup.

WALKING MAN: Thank you, you're a good friend. There aren't many like you these days.

WAITING MAN: We used to laugh vigorously.

WALKING MAN: We used to.

II

Father of WAITING MAN enters, an old sick man writhing in pain.

NARRATOR: *(To audience.)* And while the man waiting on the bed thinks that his disappeared lover is on her way to him with a fine leather suitcase, thinking only of him, in fact the person really thinking of him is his elderly father, who lives two blocks away and is lying alone, very ill, without his son knowing.

FATHER OF WAITING MAN: Very ill or dying?

NARRATOR: That will become clear this very night. *(Enter MOTHER OF WALKING MAN.)* *(The NARRATOR continues, to audience.)* Meanwhile, in the last few minutes there has been no change with the aged mother of the walking man. She is still dying.

MOTHER OF WALKING MAN: Before you said 'critically ill.'

NARRATOR: Let's call a spade a spade.

MOTHER OF WALKING MAN: I…don't believe it. I'm afraid. *(She begins to whimper, then stops.)* I…if they take me to the hospital, maybe they can still…

NARRATOR: Maybe. But you're alone, too weak to call for help.

MOTHER OF WALKING MAN: I have a son. He lives nearby.

NARRATOR: You're too weak to call him.

MOTHER OF WALKING MAN: Maybe he'll wake up suddenly and come.

NARRATOR: Maybe. *(To FATHER OF WAITING MAN, who is looking at him again.)* Maybe. *(MOTHER OF WALKING MAN and FATHER OF WAITING MAN wheeze and writhe in a sort of dialogue.)*

MOTHER OF WALKING MAN:
Gone are the days of influenza, a mild cough, a fever.
Now is the night that no day will follow.
The feet are still here
But the eyes look to that past.
Put a hand to my forehead

To wipe the sweat or for one final farewell touch.
Soon, soon, very soon.

III

WALKING MAN: *(To WAITING MAN.)* I am here to take you along with me on an expansive journey on the matter of the business I cannot divulge to you at present.

WAITING MAN: I, of course, have already been on an expansive journey and of course I do not willingly leave a warm bed with a breathing lover with cascading hair, but of course I have been waiting for this and I will come with you.

WALKING MAN: I see we have an understanding. I'll wait for you to dress.

WAITING MAN: I'm dressed.

WALKING MAN: I'll wait for you to pack a suitcase.

WAITING MAN: My suitcase is packed. You caught me with one foot out the door.

WALKING MAN: I'll wait for you to kiss your warm-bodied lover with the cascading hair.

WAITING MAN: She is spending the night at a friend's.

WALKING MAN: And the hair?

WAITING MAN: The hair she took with her.

(Pause.)

WALKING MAN: Was that a crow calling?

WAITING MAN: No, a stomach grumbling.

WALKING MAN: Something is occurring in the universe.

WAITING MAN: Yes, in this universe things are happening.
(To himself.) And if I am asked by myself why I went, I
will answer: A grown man came to call me in the dead
of night, a man who can be presumed to know what he's
doing, and I went with him for certain very important
purposes – though this is not the place to elaborate – which
will be very beneficial to me, especially in the long term.

And beneath that, I will secretly whisper to myself that a
wide-scale surprise is being planned for me with regard to
my departed love. *(They walk.)*

IV

WALKING MAN and WAITING MAN walk.

NARRATOR *(To audience.)* Each person and their shreds of
thought, characters, memories, yearnings, follies, threads
and trifles, sometimes new, mostly old, at times alone and
other times in pairs… Here, for example, the Walking
Man's quartet of timeworn thoughts.

*(Enter PICKLED HERRING THOUGHT, ASS THOUGHT, VAGUE
THOUGHT and MURKY THOUGHT.)*

PICKLED HERRING THOUGHT: Greetings, I am the
hankering for pickled herring.

ASS THOUGHT: I am the passion for ass.

VAGUE THOUGHT: And I would like to say something, too…
something important is trying to break through…

MURKY THOUGHT: And I am the memory of the
kindergarten teacher and the pail.

(They straggle a little behind the WALKING MAN and exit.)

Act Three: Evasive Man

I

Street. WALKING MAN and WAITING MAN are walking with their suitcases in the darkness.

WAITING MAN: Such darkness.

WALKING MAN: Meanwhile we can take a look at the view.

WAITING MAN: Too dark to see anything.

WALKING MAN: Darkness is a nocturnal landscape. *(They continue walking.)* Ah, to be in wide-open spaces, to breathe deeply…

WAITING MAN: They say exhaling is more important than inhaling.

WALKING MAN: Is your area divided into cantons?

WAITING MAN: Why?

WALKING MAN: Because I thought I saw lights flickering, and a laughing woman said something in Italian and a moment later we passed by a restaurant and an elegant woman whispered something in French…

WAITING MAN: Around here women enjoy themselves in many languages.

II

WAITING MAN suddenly loses his way and bumps into a wall, and groans.

WALKING MAN: What happened?

189

WAITING MAN: Nothing. *(He scans the wall, gestures to WALKING MAN to move back.)* You wait there. I have urgent business here but this is not the time or place to elaborate.

WALKING MAN: *(As if in on the information.)* I fully understand.

(WALKING MAN steps back, sits on his suitcase. WAITING MAN stands facing the wall, taps on it as if reluctant to disturb anyone, stops.)

WAITING MAN: *(Whispering to the wall.)* Open up, my love!… I waited years for you and you never came!…Open up so I can come in and both of us will be eternally happy! To live beside you, to die beneath you – that is all I wish for…! *(Looks back to WALKING MAN then, to himself.)* I bumped into the wall by accident and now he thinks I have romantic interests that are mysterious, perhaps dubious, perhaps bordering on the criminal in connection with casinos in Monaco and exclusive brothels in Istanbul. *(He taps on the wall again.)* I know you're there! I know you're there with another man!…I know you're there with another man, a better one than me!…Why did you swap? How's he better than me? *(He stops.) (To himself.)* My whole life has been nothing but striving for this: that one night I would stand facing a wall.

WALKING MAN: *(To himself.)* What to do and how to live, that is the question.

WAITING MAN: *(To himself.)* When I am downtrodden I look ponderous. A passerby expects a scientific discovery from me, like finding a cure for cancer.

WALKING MAN: *(To himself.)* I would gladly stop by my mother's, I left an encyclopedia of French culture there that I've been wanting for a while…

WAITING MAN: *(Drawing near WALKING MAN.)* It's all part of the plan and going as predicted so far.

WALKING MAN: I'm monitoring the plan and I give you permission to continue. *(To himself.)* Now he has no idea what's going on, and it occurs to him that I am the commander of a secret operation he knows nothing about. *(To WAITING MAN.)* Remind me which canton we're in; the French one?

WAITING MAN: Something like that.

III

WAITING MAN returns to the wall, knocks.

WAITING MAN: Open up, it's me!…Open, open!… *(EVASIVE MAN appears from behind the wall with a suitcase, trying to slip away. WAITING MAN rushes to stop him.)*

WAITING MAN: Slipping away?

EVASIVE MAN: *(Startled.)* Who's slipping away? Just living!

WAITING MAN: And there inside, just living?

EVASIVE MAN: Who's living? And what inside? It's just a courtyard, I went in because… I was looking around…

WAITING MAN: You were screwing, and now you're out for some fresh night air before bed!

EVASIVE MAN: *(Considering, to himself.)* They think I'm living it up with a whole whorehouse of high-class broads in my pocket. *(He puffs himself up.)* I won't deny it, I was screwing.

WAITING MAN: Who? So-and-so?

EVASIVE MAN: Who else?!

WAITING MAN: *(Tears of anger in his eyes.)* You robbed me of my beloved!

191

EVASIVE MAN: *(Fearful, to himself.)* This man looks a little dangerous to me. *(To WAITING MAN.)* Who's robbing? Who's screwing? Do I look like someone for robbing and screwing at night? I was looking for a place to pee, it was dark, I was feeling my way along the wall, there was a courtyard there, not even a dog in it, couldn't see a thing, opened my fly, all of a sudden someone knocks on the wall, didn't even have time to pee.

WAITING MAN: Tell the truth – you took her away from me! *(Turns away from him, broken.)* Were you with her? Did you love her? And she, you? Does she love you?

EVASIVE MAN: *(Scrutinizes him, to himself.)* I don't think there's any danger here.

WAITING MAN: Tell me, how was it?!

EVASIVE MAN: It was wonderful.

WAITING MAN: Did you do it... more than once?

EVASIVE MAN: *(Trying to appear nonchalant.)* I lost count.

WAITING MAN: Meaning, obviously more than twice!

EVASIVE MAN: After six I stopped counting.

WAITING MAN: Did you satisfy her? Did she come?

EVASIVE MAN: I don't know if she came or not, and I wasn't all that interested. All I know is that she screamed like mad, all kinds of things like, 'Oh my god!' and 'I can't take it anymore!' and 'I've never had anything like this before!' in French and Italian, 'Oh mon dieu, mon dieu...!'

WALKING MAN: *(Trying to eavesdrop, hearing only 'mon dieu, mon dieu', to himself.)* I see we really have crossed cantons.

EVASIVE MAN: *(Continuing.)* She had a few moans and
prayers... 'God' in French and 'God' in German and a
little song: 'On the banks of the river Rhine, I ran into
Mr. Klein' and furthermore she beat her fists on the walls,
scratched up all the paint, went wild, flipped over the bed,
tore up the sheets, knocked over the television and the
refrigerator...

WAITING MAN: You got all the way to the kitchen?!

EVASIVE MAN: I didn't even notice, I only noticed she was
nibbling on my hat.

WAITING MAN: You were screwing with your hat on?

EVASIVE MAN: My dear sir, I hardly bothered to open my
fly...

WAITING MAN: That wild?!

EVASIVE MAN: As you know.

WAITING MAN: And how is she?

EVASIVE MAN: I won't expound.

WAITING MAN: But you're tired and satisfied?

EVASIVE MAN: Thoroughly. She sucked it all out of me.

WAITING MAN: When you say 'sucked'...

EVASIVE MAN: I may have said that as a poetic image, I may
not have...I will only insinuate that in this case I would
not bet on a poetic image, and I shall not expound further
with concrete details.

WAITING MAN: You know you're torturing me?!

EVASIVE MAN: Really? By telling you how while she was
sucking she grunted like a bear, she and her two friends,
the black woman and the Norwegian one?

WAITING MAN: What?!

EVASIVE MAN: I will not expound.

WAITING MAN: They were sucking, too?

EVASIVE: I may have said that as a poetic image and I may not have. I went through maybe ten pinecones.

WAITING MAN: Pinecones as a poetic image?

EVASIVE MAN: What poetic? They only use organic vibrators… from nature. I was rubbing pinecones left and right in there, I still have the scent of natural pine resin in my nostrils. In short: Nice spending time with you guys.

WAITING MAN: *(On the verge of tears.)* She cheated on me and fell in love with you.

EVASIVE MAN: C'est la vie.

WAITING MAN: Tell me it was all a lie.

EVASIVE MAN: Sorry, I would like to, but the truth will not allow it.

WAITING MAN: Tell me it's a lie!

EVASIVE MAN: I will not. I have a life, too. I will not give it up. I will not let you take this wonderful story away from me, how on such-and-such a night…

WALKING MAN: *(To himself, upon hearing only the final words that were shouted.)* …in such-and-such a canton…

EVASIVE MAN: I screwed so-and-so with a black woman and a Norwegian and she ate my hat, and flipped over the refrigerator, and pinecones were flying. I won't give it up! I want to live and do things, too!

WAITING MAN: If that's the case, goodbye. I don't believe anything you say, I won't even remember you.

EVASIVE MAN: Who cares if you remember me? *(He exits. Returns. Pause.)* Leave me with your belief in my story.

WAITING MAN: No.

EVASIVE MAN: Believe me on the screwing and the pinecones and I'll let the fridge and the hat go.

WAITING MAN: No.

EVASIVE MAN: Okay, no pinecones.

WAITING MAN: No nothing.

EVASIVE MAN: What, not even the screwing?

WAITING MAN: No screwing.

EVASIVE MAN: What's left?

WAITING MAN: The pissing and the suitcase.

EVASIVE MAN: To be believed about the pissing and the suitcase, the whole deal isn't worth it for me. *(Exits. Returns.)* Drop the pissing but the suitcase stays.

WAITING MAN: All right.

EVASIVE MAN: And add a large member.

WAITING MAN: If you admit that you weren't screwing and you weren't doing anything, and there's no woman in there, and that you were just feeling your way along the wall, and you tried to pee and you came out – I'll believe you about the suitcase, I'll drop the pissing, and I'll add on a large member.

EVASIVE MAN: We have a deal. I wasn't screwing and there was no woman. I was walking in the dark, feeling my way along the wall, I opened my fly to pee and came back.

WAITING MAN: Your member is not small.

EVASIVE MAN: Thank you. You're a generous man.

WAITING MAN: You, too, are a worthy man.

EVASIVE MAN: *(To himself.)* In his heart of hearts he's leaving me with an option for screwing after all.

WAITING MAN: *(To himself.)* It's true, I certainly am retaining the option of seeing him as a great man and a stupendous lover who took my only love.

EVASIVE MAN: So, good night then.

WAITING MAN: Sweet dreams.

EVASIVE MAN: *(Moving to leave, then returning.)* Actually, I could join you, my second and third night shifts happen to be free.

WAITING MAN: *(To himself.)* This is good, because now my friend so-and-so standing back there will think that so-and-so standing here was waiting for me behind the wall to join me on some shady operation – maybe drugs, maybe hookers, maybe gambling… *(To EVASIVE MAN.)* Why not?

(WAITING MAN and EVASIVE MAN move to WALKING MAN. EVASIVE MAN, surprised, regards WALKING MAN.)

EVASIVE MAN: *(To himself.)* Now that guy's going to think I'm in on some mysterious, shady conspiracy with this guy, plus living it up behind the wall and maybe even a kinky nightclub.

WALKING MAN: *(To himself.)* He probably thinks I'm supervising a nighttime plan that includes the two of them, and in any event I'm certainly a big unknown to him.

WAITING MAN: *(Introducing them.)* So-and-so, meet so-and-so.

WALKING MAN: *(Eyeing EVASIVE MAN; to himself.)* Now he thinks I'm studying him carefully but he doesn't know that in fact I just want to see what a face looks like when it's hoping for something from me.

EVASIVE MAN: *(He, too, draws his face near WALKING MAN; to himself.)* Ditto.

WALKING MAN: *(Gapes at him; to himself.)* And now he's waiting to hear what will come out of my mouth. He thinks it's going to be something huge. It's a good thing there are people other than me in the world, because fooling myself is getting harder and harder.

EVASIVE MAN: *(Gapes at him; to himself.)* Ditto.

WAITING MAN: *(To himself.)* And although I know for sure that it's pointless to expect anything from these two idiots, even a used bus ticket, I still have great, exhilarating hope from these two exalted people for unexpected joy with my vanished lover. *(They walk.)*

IV

Enter VAGUE THOUGHT and MURKY THOUGHT, arguing.

MURKY THOUGHT: I remember the kindergarten teacher and the pail.

VAGUE THOUGHT: But I would like to say, there's something pressing, something important needs to come out, if only I had a moment's quiet to find the word… if only I weren't surrounded by insipidness…

MURKY THOUGHT: I remember the kindergarten teacher and the pail.

(Enter ASS THOUGHT and PICKLED HERRING THOUGHT.)

PICKLED HERRING THOUGHT: Pickled herring, my learned friend, pickled herring.

ASS THOUGHT: Allow me, dear colleague: ass.

PICKLED HERRING THOUGHT: On an empty stomach?

ASS THOUGHT: Well how else, on a full stomach, with all the blood busy digesting the pickled herring?

PICKLED HERRING THOUGHT: Man, how much blood does it take for a piece of pickled herring?

ASS THOUGHT: And going straight for the ass with your breath stinking of herring?

PICKLED HERRING THOUGHT: As if an asshole smells like chrysanthemums…

ASS THOUGHT: Yes, but who expects that from an ass?

PICKLED HERRING THOUGHT: Why is it not expected from an ass yet it is from pickled herring?

ASS THOUGHT: Oy, having a conversation with you…

PICKLED HERRING THOUGHT: Moreover, with pickled herring you get right to the point. But with a woman, god help you…

ASS THOUGHT: On the other hand, with pickled herring *you* have to wash the dishes afterward, whereas with an ass, *she* does the washing.

PICKLED HERRING THOUGHT: You were, and always will be, a degenerate.

MURKY THOUGHT: I remember the kindergarten teacher and the pail.

VAGUE THOUGHT: Oy, if only I had a moment's quiet.

(Enter LAJAN THOUGHT, dressed as a beautiful French university student.)

NARRATOR: In our city, another thought has recently been wandering the streets: abstract, complex, the latest word in post-modernist theory à la the elderly professor Lajan. She is beautiful, bold, heavenly, refined, contemplated by young students with long straight hair on autumn nights in Paris…

(ASS THOUGHT and PICKLED HERRING THOUGHT approach her.)

ASS THOUGHT: I want so badly to cling to you, sometimes it's suffocating, sometimes one wishes to rise above the superficiality, the crudeness, to forget the flesh, to penetrate loftier spheres. Sometimes one has dreams that one has no strength to fulfill. My wonderful, spiritual, airy, slender one…!

PICKLED HERRING THOUGHT: Pickled herring, what else is there to say, it's only pickled herring. And yet, I permit myself… I'm not saying, after all, I do come from the bottom… and yet… there may be a stench of fish but the heart soars to the horizon… just think what a wonderful match we could be, the pickled and the transcendent, post-modernism and mackerel, you and me…!

LAJAN THOUGHT: Who are *you*? I'm from the Sorbonne!

ASS THOUGHT: I'm from the undies.

PICKLED HERRING THOUGHT: I'm from the barrel.

LAJAN THOUGHT: I promenade about the Luxembourg gardens and Saint Germain, I sit at café de Flore and Brasserie Lipp, I sleep in Passy, I will die in Neuilly and I will be buried in Père Lachaise. And you?

ASS THOUGHT: We live in the pits…

PICKLED HERRING THOUGHT: And we'll be buried in the gutter…

ASS THOUGHT: But we dream of Paris.

LAJAN THOUGHT: I'm a little busy. *(She exits.)*

ASS THOUGHT: Excuse us...

PICKLED HERRING THOUGHT: And au revoir. *(They follow after her.)*

WALKING MAN: *(To himself.)* I am wondering whether there is any point in going now, in the middle of the night, to pick up a dusty old French encyclopedia...

VAGUE THOUGHT: If only the conditions were right, if only I had a little quiet, a moment of concentration, I could finally lift off above this terrible banality, I would sparkle above the world with a profound, original idea that no one has yet conceived...

MURKY THOUGHT: I remember the kindergarten teacher...

VAGUE THOUGHT *(In desperation.)* Good god!

(They exit. WALKING MAN, WAITING MAN and EVASIVE MAN continue walking.)

Act Four: Walkers in the Dark

I

WALKING MAN, WAITING MAN and EVASIVE MAN stop.

WALKING MAN: *(To WAITING MAN.)* Where are we?

WAITING MAN: In terms of canton or in terms of street?

WALKING MAN: In terms of canton.

WAITING MAN: In terms of canton we're in such-and-such.

WALKING MAN: I know, I was just making sure.

(They continue walking.)

II

NARRATOR:

And meanwhile, with so many lofty thoughts and hopes
suspended above the dark streets of our city, our old
acquaintances re-enter our story, dying alone in their beds,
alone in their homes. *(Enter MOTHER OF WALKING MAN and
FATHER OF WAITING MAN.)* They are then joined by the
possibly-dead, possibly-in-Canada mother of the evasive
man. *(Enter two old women, one dead, one alive.)* These are
two women who do not know one another, but because
the evasive man was given up for adoption as a baby
and does not know to this day whether his true mother is
living in Canada or is dead, we are obliged to welcome
both into our story.

MOTHER OF WALKING MAN: *(To NARRATOR.)* I want to see my son... he'll call an ambulance... he will put a hand to my forehead... kind man, help me call my son...

NARRATOR: Please understand that I can do nothing for you, I am only the narrator of this story, I am wind, air, I have no power to move even a crumb, only to describe you all, and the night, and your walking in the dark, and your passions and your groans, and your calls for help, and your demise. Please understand...

MOTHER OF WALKING MAN: He is my son... I gave birth to him... he must come.

WALKING MAN: *(To himself.)* Maybe I will stop by her place after all, I'll take the encyclopedia and flip through it tonight... they won't know where I've snuck off to and they'll think I've got some big mysterious meeting.

MOTHER OF WALKING MAN: My son...my son... he'll come...

FATHER OF WAITING MAN: *(To NARRATOR.)* And me, will I live to see morning?

NARRATOR: Seems not.

FATHER OF WAITING MAN: Dying, then.

NARRATOR: Yes.

FATHER OF WAITING MAN: *(Draws near MOTHER OF WALKING MAN. The two wheeze, struggling to breathe.)* Oh, old lady, I've never met you, I don't even know your name, but now, in all the universe you are the person closest to me; one thread, unseen yet stronger than any other, ties us together. We could blend our final breaths and take flight together over the world and its follies, over the banks,

202

the hospitals, the revolutions in South America, and listen attentively hand in hand to the breaths, one... and another... and another...

IV

NARRATOR *(To audience.)* Do not think that while these two are dying, the dead parents of the dying old lady and the dead parents of the dying old man aren't rotting away each in their own grave in the nearby city cemetery, lying there, each corpse in its own slow decay among the other graves. *(Enter the dead parents of WALKING MAN's mother and the dead parents of WAITING MAN's father. THE NARRATOR introduces WALKING MAN'S DYING MOTHER to her own dead parents.)* You loved her once. Look what's become of your little girl. She is old, worn out, dying, the end. *(The dead parents do not react. To the audience.)* Uninterested. The pure egotism of the dead.

(Enter TRIVIAL MAN and his mother.)

NARRATOR: You've already been told *no*, Trivial Man and Trivial Dead Mother of Trivial Man.

MOTHER OF TRIVIAL MAN: I was thinking of popping up in a memory, but I won't insist. Loneliness is not all that bad. I do not exist, Ladies and Gentlemen, I do not. I cannot be hurt, insulted, abandoned... *(The tears begin to roll down her face.)* I can no longer feel pain, because I am not here, I do not feel a thing, I'm beyond it all, the loneliness and the nonexistence have become a constant ringing that turns over time into part of the silence. You cannot know it, you cannot imagine it, until you, too, get there.

(TRIVIAL MAN and his mother exit. The dead parents of WALKING MAN's mother and WAITING MAN's father are joined by a long line of dead people.)

NARRATOR: Ladies and Gentlemen, not tonight! Please, I beg you, ladies and gentlemen…!

(He tries to push them out, in vain. They squabble among themselves, calling out to the audience.)

TIRED DEAD MAN: So-and-so. From such-and-such year to such-and-such year.

DILIGENT DEAD MAN: Born so-and-so, I changed it overseas to such-and-such. I returned home as so-and-so. Son of so-and-so.

BITTER DEAD WOMAN: His wife. Née such-and-such. Daughter of so-and-so.

SHY DEAD MAN: So-and-so. And I would like to say…

GENTLE DEAD WOMAN: So-and-so. I didn't live, and I can do nothing but draw your attention to such-and-such.

ANGRY DEAD MAN: All this such-and-such-and-so-and-so-and-such-and-such… How come we can't lie here and dream here in peace?

BITTER DEAD WOMAN: What would you dream about?

ANGRY DEAD MAN: What does anyone dream about? Women, mackerel, and the messiah!

VULGAR DEAD MAN: 'Women!' And you still have your tongue?!

DESPAIRING DEAD MAN: Oh, nonsense, always quarreling, always the same old story. The hell with you!

DEAD TOT: Child. So-and-so-y.

SOUR DEAD WOMAN: Of a grave illness, young, never married. So-and-so, such-and-such year to such-and-such year.

SHY DEAD MAN: And I would like to say…

ANGRY DEAD MAN: Enough, gentlemen, enough speaking, you've said enough! A little quiet. A little dreaming.

VULGAR DEAD MAN: And you, what's wrong with you? Always shutting everyone's mouths!

ANGRY DEAD MAN: What's wrong with me is what's wrong with me, sir, I'm not in here for haemorrhoids, I'm in for death.

BITTER DEAD WOMAN: I'm not exactly here for a blister, either! Everyone's in here for death, sir.

ANGRY DEAD MAN: We've heard all about you. Women! You're not dead at all, you're just crawling through the center of the earth in a tunnel to Australia and opening up whorehouses!

BITTER DEAD WOMAN: And what about you men? Lying with your mouths open looking up widows' dresses!

ANGRY DEAD MAN: How could we possibly look? We're covered in dirt!

BITTER DEAD WOMAN: They bury you with periscopes!

DESPAIRING DEAD MAN: Oh, to hell with them, not a moment's peace! And this is who I have to build a cemetery with?!

ANGRY DEAD MAN: What does it take to get some peace around here?!

VULGAR DEAD MAN: Pffffffff!

DESPAIRING DEAD MAN: Oh, to hell with it!

ANGRY DEAD MAN: Quiet!!!

VULGAR DEAD MAN: Get over here, I'll show you…!

ANGRY DEAD MAN: You get over here, I'm not scared of you!

VULGAR DEAD MAN: Come on, come on, let's see you!

ANGRY DEAD MAN: No, you get over here!

VULGAR DEAD MAN: Over there you're a big talker! Lying on your back for twenty years shouting 'Get over here!'

ANGRY DEAD MAN: Because I'm shouting 'Get over here!' and you're not coming!

VULGAR DEAD MAN: And I shout 'Get over here!' and you *are* coming?!

ANGRY DEAD MAN: First let's see you get over here, then I'll get over there!

DESPAIRING DEAD MAN: Oh, to hell with you! How'd I end up here? Serves me right for dying with a bunch of Middle Easterners!

VULGAR DEAD MAN: Pffffff.

ANGRY DEAD MAN: Australia!

BITTER DEAD WOMAN: Periscopes!

DESPAIRING DEAD MAN: I should have been buried in Vienna!

VULGAR DEAD MAN: Do me a favor, people, you have here a classical musician, very sensitive! Pffffff!

DESPAIRING DEAD MAN: Filth! Always with the filth! And the noise, the noise! Day after day, cantors and widows and tractors and contractors; the widow quiets down – the tractor rattles; the tractor rolls off – an airplane buzzes; the airplane disappears – a phone rings…! Oh, how sick we are of this cursed Orient: dust, flies, noise! What a commotion over a little dust! At night, the markets up

there shut down and the goings-on down here start up:
'You get over here!' 'Let's see you: you get over here!'
Good god, you promised us after death we would rest in
peace; where's the rest and where's the peace? To hell
with it, I should have been buried in Vienna.

MOTHER OF THE MOTHER: Having retired from the world,
as we did, we should have been able to spend our
time in the grave together, having a quiet party, slowly
disintegrating, making the occasional soft sound, like the
slight creaking of furniture at night...

FATHER OF THE MOTHER: And it's a pity. So many men and
women, all available, with plenty of time, to wonder what
our lives were, and why...

*(Someone begins to sing, another to shout. They leave in a din of
quarreling.)*

V

*Enter ASS THOUGHT, PICKLED HERRING THOUGHT, VAGUE
THOUGHT, MURKY THOUGHT. They encounter TROUSER THOUGHT,
CHOCOLATE THOUGHT, PYRAMID THOUGHT. PICKLED HERRING
THOUGHT turns to CHOCOLATE THOUGHT.*

PICKLED HERRING THOUGHT *(To a THOUGHT that looks like
it.)* Excuse me, are you so-and-so's thought about pickled
herring?

CHOCOLATE THOUGHT: No, I'm so-and-so's thought about
chocolate; *that* is the thought about pickled herring. But not
so-and-so's – such-and-such's, right next to the thought
about pyramids. So-and-so's pickled herring thought is
over there, with the thought about new gabardine trousers.

TROUSER THOUGHT: I am the thought about gabardine
trousers, but not so-and-so's, such-and-such's. So-and-so's

pickled herring thought stepped out for a moment with the thought about life's follies, she should be back any moment. Was it something urgent?

PICKLED HERRING THOUGHT: No, just an exchange of opinions.

VAGUE THOUGHT: If only you would all keep quiet for a moment... let me lift off...

MURKY THOUGHT: I remember the kindergarten teacher and the pail.

VAGUE THOUGHT: What was in that pail?

MURKY THOUGHT: The kindergarten teacher.

VAGUE THOUGHT: What was she doing?

MURKY THOUGHT: She was in the pail.

VAGUE THOUGHT: Let me lift off... something important is trying to break through...

(Enter LAJAN THOUGHT.)

ASS THOUGHT: My cherished one, my heart's desire...

PICKLED HERRING THOUGHT: And what about me?

LAJAN THOUGHT: You must understand, we have nothing in common. Of the lot of you, I'd prefer him.

(She points at PYRAMID THOUGHT.)

PYRAMID THOUGHT: Hello. I am the thought about pyramids.

LAJAN THOUGHT: Even though he's not much of a theory either. But still, pyramids, not a derriere.

PYRAMID THOUGHT: That's true, there's something cultured about me, something historical, spiritual...

PICKLED HERRING THOUGHT: What do you mean 'spiritual'? What exactly do you *think* about pyramids?

PYRAMID THOUGHT: I just think. Pyramids. That's all.

PICKLED HERRING THOUGHT: What's the big deal. You're not actually making any intellectual effort. You're just like me. I could have thought about pyramids instead of pickled herring, too.

PYRAMID THOUGHT: You could have, that's true, except that I grabbed it first. I'm happy: I get culture and I don't work hard.

WALKING MAN: *(To himself.)* And what would be the point of stopping by my mother's now just to schlepp French encyclopedias in the middle of the night. That's ridiculous… I'll pick them up another time…

(He continues walking with WAITING MAN and EVASIVE MAN.)

VI

Suddenly WAITING MAN turns back, runs to the wall, pounds on it and shouts.

WAITING MAN: Open up, it's me…! Open up! Open so that my walking shall have a purpose, and so that the world will know that I have a beloved, and the world is real, and I wasn't born for no reason… If I've done something wrong, I will make amends. I'll change, I'll be a different man, tall and cheerful, insightful, humorous, unceasingly vivacious… I will demand nothing of you… I will not consummate my love for you… at most we will get engaged, I won't touch you, I'll observe you from afar… Come back for an hour, for a minute, then leave… See what rivers of filth I pass through just to preserve something of my dignity… I cannot go back without you, please understand, I am here with people, they believe me… my words have some value… *(Bashes his head against the wall, stops.)* How will I justify this night? What will I tell them? How will I justify this dark, draining, dreadful night? What will I do with myself from here on? What will I tell them? What will I do? *(Pause. His head still to the wall; to himself.)* The hardest thing, when I turn to look back at them, is how to keep from swallowing. And that is the problem, the problem of all problems: how to conceal the movement of the Adam's apple during the greatest humiliation of your life. *(Turning to WALKING MAN and EVASIVE MAN, trying to sound casual.)* So how about that revolution in Nicaragua? Any news? *(He stops, clears his throat, tries to fight back tears, starts humming.)* Zing-a-ling, zing-a-ling, Honey in the moonshine… *(He stops, waves dismissively toward the wall.)* She isn't even pretty, isn't pretty… *(He stops, again, casually.)* And I mean, it's all of Latin America… and we all remember what happened in El Salvador… *(He stops, waves dismissively again.)* She isn't pretty, isn't pretty, and her hair doesn't even… *(The words get caught in his throat. WALKING MAN approaches him and lays a hand on his shoulder.)*

WALKING MAN: The situation in Nicaragua is truly catastrophic.

WAITING MAN: *(No longer able to control the wave of tears overwhelming him. WALKING MAN stands helplessly.)* Help me!

WALKING MAN: One day we'll die, nothing will be left of the heartbreak and the shame…

WAITING MAN: Help me!

(Enter MOTHER OF WALKING MAN, breathing heavily. NARRATOR listens tensely to her breathing.)

WALKING MAN: All will be forgotten, as if it had never existed…

WAITING MAN: Help me!

NARRATOR: Shhhhh… Death.

WALKING MAN: *(Turning from WAITING MAN to NARRATOR.)* Not yet. She'll only die at dawn. So that while I'm walking at night with my suitcase, with my longings and my trifling contemplations, and my aspiration to leave a mark as a man who knows what he's doing – my mother will be dying, the woman whose breath was the first human breath I inhaled, her pleasant, tranquil breath now taken from her, from the foul-smelling, shriveled old hag so far removed from that other woman as to be wholly unrelated… it all somehow slipped away without us noticing… *(Begins to cry, then pushes on.)* But as of yet I do not know, I will only know tomorrow morning. For now I am with my friends, in the dark, on the street, with a suitcase. And not only do I not suspect anything, but – *(Singing.)* Zing-a-ling, zing-a-ling – *(To WAITING MAN.)* I am suddenly overwhelmed with happiness.

WAITING MAN: Just like that?

WALKING MAN: Just like that, no reason, one of those moments of joy that suddenly flares up without knowing why. *(He sings for a moment with WAITING MAN, then stops.)* Oops! Happiness gone.

WAITING MAN: *(Gradually stops crying, a sheepish grin on his face.)* And yet I have hope. Sometimes a man says, 'The laws of nature won't work here. Some sort of miracle is in order.' A miracle is what I need.

MOTHER OF WALKING MAN: *(To NARRATOR.)* But when will he come? Time is running out…

WAITING MAN: *(To EVASIVE MAN.)* And you, you were lying. What were you really doing behind that wall?

EVASIVE MAN: Who can say who's been lying? The nights are dark, and life is built on a story built of words: one speaks, the others listen.

VII

Enter VAGUE THOUGHT and MURKY THOUGHT.

VAGUE THOUGHT: I know what you're going to say.

MURKY THOUGHT: I remember the kindergarten teacher and the pail.

VAGUE THOUGHT: Good god.

MURKY THOUGHT: I know what you're going to say, too: How tired we are of each other.

VAGUE THOUGHT *(Teary-eyed.)* When will you all give me some peace? When will you understand that something incomparably important is hovering on the tip of my tongue?

MURKY THOUGHT: She was standing in the pail, with her back to me, in a light-gray swimsuit, and I was behind her, watching…

(Enter ASS THOUGHT and PICKLED HERRING THOUGHT, who encounter LAJAN THOUGHT arm-in-arm with PYRAMID THOUGHT.)

ASS THOUGHT: So I'm not going to get you, am I?

LAJAN THOUGHT: You're ugly.

ASS THOUGHT: What can I do?

LAJAN THOUGHT: And you're rude.

ASS THOUGHT: That's true.

LAJAN THOUGHT: And you are shallow and primitive and naïve, and practically an imbecile...

ASS THOUGHT: A lost cause, eh?

LAJAN THOUGHT: And you intrigue me.

ASS THOUGHT *(Astonished.)* Excuse me?

LAJAN THOUGHT: And you...amuse me.

ASS THOUGHT: I do?

LAJAN THOUGHT: That wild spark in your eyes.

ASS THOUGHT: Am I hearing right?

LAJAN THOUGHT: And your lips, I liked them right from the start.

ASS THOUGHT: The French women have lost their minds. *(She caresses his hair.)* I don't believe it.

LAJAN THOUGHT *(Embracing him.)* And now?

ASS THOUGHT: Not yet.

LAJAN THOUGHT *(Kissing him softly.)* And now?

ASS THOUGHT: A little.

LAJAN THOUGHT: I like your voice. The gruffness.

ASS THOUGHT: It's not gruff, it's nasal.

LAJAN THOUGHT: It doesn't bother me. *(ASS THOUGHT coughs.)* And it doesn't bother me that you have a cold and you haven't brushed your teeth. *(She kisses him again.)*

ASS THOUGHT: You're incredible. And I am breathless.

LAJAN THOUGHT: I know, I may be a literary theory and all that, but even the ass is no stranger to us theories! Come!

PYRAMID THOUGHT: Whores! *(He exits.)*

WALKING MAN: *(To himself.)* I think I'll stop by my mother's house after all and pick up the French encyclopedia. A little riffle through French culture before bed could only help matters…

PICKLED HERRING THOUGHT *(To himself.)* Meanwhile, the pickled herring has been forgotten. I shall never be privileged to penetrate French culture, I will never be like family to them, I will only peer in longingly from the threshold, turn back and return to my homeland to be what I am: a godforsaken oriental thought about Polish pickled herring.

VIII

WALKING MAN, WAITING MAN and EVASIVE MAN trudge along. EVASIVE MAN hums sourly to himself.

EVASIVE MAN: Strung along time's thread are we, out the hole from where you pee… *(Walking man and WAITING MAN begin to laugh and horse around.)*

WALKING MAN: Someone peering at us through the slats of a shuttered window must be saying to himself we're some kind of big deal. An entire city is sleeping peacefully–

WAITING MAN: …including lovers with cascading hair…

WALKING MAN: …while three brave, tough agents work tirelessly to keep it safe…

WAITING MAN: …and indeed, who can say whether we aren't such men…

EVASIVE MAN: *(Grumbling to himself.)* I was on my way home after a nighttime meander following the usual boredom before bed, I stopped to pee behind a wall and now suddenly I find myself running through dark streets with god-knows-who out of some hope that this has to do with international prostitution, because I have no affinity for drugs and espionage, but all in all I would gladly give up this running around for a hot cup of tea, a pee, and to bed.

(From the other side of the stage, in a tight single file, enter SQUEEZING MAN 1, SQUEEZING MAN 2, SQUEEZING MAN 3. The two groups stand looking at one another for a moment.)

WALKING MAN: *(To himself.)* What I would feel like saying, more than anything else, if we were truly talking to one another, is this *(WALKING MAN, EVASIVE MAN and WAITING MAN draw near the others.)* Where are you from?

SQUEEZING MAN:1: From there.

WALKING MAN: Is it good there?

SQUEEZING MAN:1: No. It's not good there. And you?

WALKING MAN: From there.

SQUEEZING MAN:1: Is it good there?

WALKING MAN: No, it's not good there.

WAITING MAN: Have you seen a woman?

SQUEEZING MAN:2: We weren't born yesterday.

WALKING MAN: And why in the dead of night? And why so squeezed together?

SQUEEZING MAN:1: We're squeezing our way to urgently becoming other people, people whose suitcases gather dust in an attic, people who sleep at night in briefs next to a woman…

215

SQUEEZING MAN:3: …with long hair cascading on a white pillow.

WAITING MAN: Oh, her hair!

SQUEEZING MAN:3: The long hair cascading over her shoulders, tickling our nostrils.

WAITING MAN: I was particularly impressed with the tickling while casually breathing.

SQUEEZING MAN:1: Yes, listen, to be beyond it all, all the dramas, the struggle, the tension, the searching, just lying with a woman and breathing casually; that is happiness. That is the quiet river of life.

SQUEEZING MAN:3: I particularly liked the full hair. I don't like a woman with thin hair. I like a lot. Thighs, too. Not in terms of hair, in terms of volume. Butter cookies, too. Not one or two, a whole package.

SQUEEZING MAN:1: And chocolate covered.

SQUEEZING MAN:2: I was the personal coiffeur of the duchess of Argenson.

WAITING MAN: What's she like?

SQUEEZING MAN:2: Pretty and bad-tempered.

WAITING MAN: Mine, too. I really like that type.

SQUEEZING MAN:3: That stunning bounty of women with the greatest potential to inflict pain.

WAITING MAN: Mine, too. She's spending the night at… well, it's a matter upon which I cannot elaborate for obvious reasons. If you see her, report to me immediately.

SQUEEZING MAN:1: I'm a great believer in if only I had this and that I'd have been such-and-such long ago, and that seeing as I do not have this and that, I'm done for.

WALKING MAN: You've broken my heart. It's not even dawn yet, the driver of the first bus is still dreaming, and you're already squeezing your way. People, you're breaking my heart. At night, hearts break. Like fine china, they tinkle, they crack, they shatter into shards. And who shall piece them together? Proud and noble, the earth sails the expanse like a royal flagship with us on the deck, craning our necks to see: Where are we? What is our destination? Come with me!

SQUEEZING MAN:1 *(To SQUEEZING MAN 3.)* He talks so deep you can't understand him.

SQUEEZING MAN:3: That man arouses great faith in me.

SQUEEZING MAN:1: I particularly like the sailing ship.

SQUEEZING MAN:3: What *I* like best on deck is a woman with long hair waving in the wind. *(Whimpering.)* I so want to be a different man!

(SQUEEZING MAN 1 and SQUEEZING MAN 3 turn to join WALKING MAN. SQUEEZING MAN 2 whispers in their direction.)

SQUEEZING MAN:2: What kind of bill of goods is he trying to sell us? He'll take us, he'll spin us around, and in the end he'll sell us rotten tins of sardines or used razor blades. *(Shouting.)* On my tombstone they'll write, 'Didn't live, didn't have fun, was mired in muck, ended up as nothing.' But one thing they won't be able to write is 'Was cheated'! No, gentlemen, not me. Please bury me with a look of suspicion and skepticism! Not resignation, not torment, but great suspicion!

EVASIVE MAN: *(To SQUEEZING MAN 2.)* Do you know you're my reflection? Perhaps I'm looking in the mirror.

SQUEEZING MAN:2: And perhaps just the opposite?

WALKING MAN: *(To himself.)* Thus would our conversation be conducted were we to talk. But perhaps it would all happen differently, perhaps we would all sing together...

ALL SIX: Strung along time's thread are we, out the hole from where you pee, spinning about athrill, like sausages on a grill...

WAITING MAN: And all the world would sing with us, and there would be a sort of shout of all humanity that would tip the earth off its course, and everyone would clutch one another to keep from falling... Oh, my beloved, where are you?

SQUEEZING MAN:1: But we are not singing and we are not speaking. We are standing, one group facing the other in silence.

WALKING MAN: At the same time I feel quite sure there was a certain summit, perhaps squandered, of something, though I myself do not know what it was.

IX

Enter THE THOUGHTS, THE DEAD and THE DYING, their numbers now doubled because they have been joined by their counterparts that belong to the Squeezing Men.

NARRATOR *(Grumbling, to the audience.)* And they, too, have mothers and fathers who have died, and they, too, have mothers and fathers who are dying now, and they, too, have shreds of thought, characters, memories, yearnings, follies, threads and trifles, sometimes new, mostly old, at times alone and other times in pairs... and these straggle behind me, oh, how vexing, what a procession I'm dragging along!

(THE LIVING and THE DEAD wave to one another.)

THE LIVING: Hey there, you who were, what do you see?

THE DEAD: Hey there, you who still are, we see nothing. Hey there, you who still are. What do you see?

THE LIVING: Hey there, you who were, we see you. Hey there, you who were, you used to be and now you're not.

THE DEAD: Hey there, you who still are, you're next.

X

MOTHER OF WALKING MAN: *(Bursting out from the crowd of THOUGHTS, THE DEAD and THE DYING.)* For one brief flickering moment, and I do not know how this keeps happening to me, I had a hope that a consortium of the finest doctors from around the world had come to cure me. For a moment I thought that the grace of God had descended upon the earth, and I was being redeemed. And I said to myself, here come three, and then another three, and they will come in threes, three angels after three angels and they will fill the street, the city, the country, and they will find my cure.

NARRATOR: Oh God, it breaks the heart to see such foolishness!

(GOD appears behind THE NARRATOR.)

GOD: Did someone call me?

NARRATOR: Me. I'm the narrator of this story.

GOD *(Chuckling.)* You're telling me? I created *you*, with this story, together.

NARRATOR: Wasn't it *me* who thought *you* up, along with the thought that *you* created *me*?

GOD: I created that thought, too.

NARRATOR: Thank you, I appreciate it. And since you're here, your honor, would you mind if I asked…

GOD: Usually I'm asked two questions: First, if I exist. Well, here I am.

NARRATOR *(Hesitant, slightly apprehensive.)* Do you maybe have some…proof?

GOD: No.

NARRATOR: Thanks, I was just asking.

GOD: And the second question is, Why did I create evil? To which I reply…

(He continues speaking, but the din of a passing train drowns out his words. The din ends.)

NARRATOR: Your honor, we didn't hear your answer to the second question because of the noise.

GOD: I will not repeat myself.

NARRATOR *(To audience, pointing to GOD.)* God! Would you believe it? A man with a suitcase, on the street, like it's nothing, no big deal, and it turns out – God. Although, as you just heard, he has no proof. And the answer to the second question? We didn't hear that, either. Because of the train. And by the way, here in our town there is no train track; could it be that God performed a magic trick and created a train for five seconds only so that it would drown out the answer to embarrassing questions? In any case, gentlemen: God.

(GOD rises, lifts his suitcase, turns to exit, then casually tosses out a riddle.)

GOD: Rhyming pair: Lovely feline.

NARRATOR: Pretty kitty.

GOD: Pretty kitty! Two points. *(Exits.)*

NARRATOR *(Calling after him.)* Wait! And the matter itself! What did you come for? And the matter itself…!

(Suddenly feels ill, nearly collapses.)

MOTHER OF WALKING MAN: What happened?

NARRATOR: I completely forgot that one day I, too, will die! Oh, how frightening! And in the grave there is no light, no air! The heart refuses to believe or the brain to grasp: one day I will be no longer! *(His legs buckle and he sits on his little suitcase.)* I am so afraid! *(Pause.)* It passed. *(He rises, scoffs. To audience.)* Oy, always the same fears, the same questions; how long shall we all say the same battered things? When will someone finally stand up and say things not yet heard?

SHY DEAD MAN: I would like to say…

(NARRATOR waves out all THE DEAD, DYING and THOUGHTS.)

XI

WALKING MAN: *(To WAITING MAN.)* Did you feel something?

WAITING MAN: A sort of sudden breeze at my back.

WALKING MAN: Autumn's arrived. Sensitive types already need a sweater at night. *(To the SQUEEZING MEN.)* We've done our job, it's time for us to walk.

SQUEEZING MAN:1: That's right. We're walking *there*, and you're walking *there*.

WAITING MAN: It's just like a changing of the guard.

WALKING MAN: You're not wrong. *(To the SQUEEZING MEN.)* Now we part. Goodbye. Things no ear has heard will yet become clear. Return to your homes and await instructions.

(The SQUEEZING MEN start to walk, then stop.)

SQUEEZING MAN:1: Gentlemen, freeze this moment, we will miss it.

(They exit. MOTHER OF WALKING MAN enters.)

MOTHER OF WALKING MAN: For one brief flickering moment… The moment has passed.

(She exits. WALKING MAN tries to keep walking, but cannot.)

WAITING MAN: What happened?

WALKING MAN: He doesn't ask me about the pain on the left side of my chest.

WAITING MAN: *(Dryly, begrudgingly.)* Oh right, what about it? Has it passed?

WALKING MAN: No, not ever *(To WAITING MAN and EVASIVE MAN.)* I think with that we've come full circle.

WAITING MAN: I also think we've come full circle and we can go back.

EVASIVE MAN: *(To himself.)* And I can finally pee at home in peace.

WALKING MAN: *(To himself.)* Everything's so strange. All of a sudden, in the midst of walking, your feet stop, you don't have the strength to take even one more step. All at once you're hit by such heavy despair that you turn to stone. Who will lift you up? Who will rescue you? Who will give you answers? *(Pause.)* Shall we go back? *(The three walk.)*

Act Five: Putting Evasive Man to Sleep

|

Enter ASS THOUGHT and LAJAN THOUGHT arm in arm. ASS THOUGHT is trying to extricate himself.

LAJAN THOUGHT: My love...

ASS THOUGHT: No, it won't work.

LAJAN THOUGHT: I love you.

ASS THOUGHT: With sorrow I tell you, Lajan's theory doesn't turn me on. I am a simple thought. Since childhood I have been carrying only myself, bearing the load, the torments, but also the pleasure. And that is how I shall remain, with myself, the burning nights of delirium, alone, in bed, with pounding heart, feverish, with palpitations and hoarse moans. I wish you the best.

LAJAN THOUGHT: Goodbye. I'm flying off to try my luck elsewhere, before I grow old.

ASS THOUGHT: Try Eastern Europe – Warsaw or Prague – they've just purged themselves of Communism.

LAJAN THOUGHT: Farewell to you, close study of the ass!

ASS THOUGHT: Farewell to you, alluring cultural musing!

LAJAN THOUGHT: Au revoir, Middle Easterners!

ASS THOUGHT: A dieu, Paris!

(Exit LAJAN THOUGHT.)

WALKING MAN: *(To himself.)* It's final: I won't get the encyclopedia tonight. I'll go straight home. To sleep, to sleep, to sleep.

(Enter PICKLED HERRING THOUGHT, who stands next to ASS THOUGHT.)

ASS THOUGHT: What more can we say about the ass that has not been said. The heavenly softness, without bones, without nuances, without psychology, without nonsense, softer than the skull, firmer than the breast, a midpoint between steel and water, and between the two sides a riverbed runs deep – oh, the painful, promising, dark crevice, the great rift valley, a place for all seasons, oh ass, sweet-and-sour suffering, a whole world unto itself, which, like our world, is also meaningless, but who cares about meaning, meaning be damned as long as it is firm and valid, standing strong!

PICKLED HERRING THOUGHT:
Who fills us with daring
Whose virtues are glaring
Who ignites us
Who incites us
Who excites us
But never bites us
Who is tasty and never goes to waste-y
Whose gills give us thrills
Which fish is the tastiest dish, everyone's wish, better than a knish
Who fills us with daring
Whose virtues are glaring
Brothers, peers,
It's pickled herring!

(The two exit.)

WALKING MAN, WAITING MAN and EVASIVE MAN are walking. They reach EVASIVE MAN's house.

EVASIVE MAN: We're back. This is my room. This is my bed.

WALKING MAN: Time to part.

(They shake hands.)

EVASIVE MAN: One last word, man to man: I was very moved when we became a community. Remember? Six of us. We could have changed the world.

WALKING MAN: The thing is, I felt great weariness. And a fog in my head. And I had to go home to rest.

EVASIVE MAN: I knew right from the start, I already suspected that all you wanted was to rest. Perhaps the need to urinate made me sharper. At any rate, I suspected.

WAITING MAN: And what did you gain from suspecting? You're standing in the same place and you're still the same idiot, so what do you get out of all this suspicion?

EVASIVE MAN: What do I get out of it? That remains to be seen. And even if it's nothing, at least they won't write 'was cheated' on my tombstone! *(WALKING MAN and WAITING MAN turn to go.)* Wait, no, wait a moment. *(They stop.)* Forgive the suspicion. The suspicion is cancelled. Starting tonight I am an innocent believer. I am different. I am an open, warm, hearty, giving man. Will you cancel my suspicion?

WALKING MAN: Suspicion cancelled.

EVASIVE MAN: But you'll leave me the big member and the option for screwing, right? Good. Then goodbye. First I'll go pee, then I'll sleep. It will be satisfying. True, this is not what I dreamt of as a child. But still, it's a life. Goodbye. *(WALKING MAN and WAITING MAN turn to leave. EVASIVE MAN begins talking again and they stop.)* The thing is, future generations will demand a reckoning. They'll ask 'For what purpose did you walk on that night, what was your life wasted on, why did you wear socks and underwear...' Future generations...

WALKING MAN: Future generations won't ask a thing. Future generations won't even remember we existed.

EVASIVE MAN: Yes, well. I'll go pee. Sadly, I am not a spiritual man. Goodbye. *(WALKING MAN and WAITING MAN turn to leave. EVASIVE MAN begins speaking again. They stop.)* And you should know...when I stand in the dark by my bed with the dirty mattress and the question is whether to lie in the sour stench of my drool, or to walk in the dark, in the terrible prolonged ringing of the silence. And what sort of a choice is that, between stench and silence... please walk me to my bed... brothers, mothers, put me to sleep, I'm tired... *(WALKING MAN and WAITING MAN put EVASIVE MAN to sleep in his bed, where he sprawls.)* Wait until I fall asleep. It'll only take a minute. I'm so tired. *(He closes his eyes. Pause.)*

WALKING MAN: He's asleep.

EVASIVE MAN: *(Opens his eyes.)* No. Can't do it. *(EVASIVE MAN'S CANADIAN MOTHER and EVASIVE MAN's Dead Mother walk past.)* And my mother? Have you found out if she's in Canada or dead?

NARRATOR: Still unknown.

EVASIVE MAN: I'll never know. *(He closes his eyes. WALKING MAN and WAITING MAN exit. EVASIVE MAN opens his eyes.)* Don't go… and life has passed…

Act Six: Putting Waiting Man to Sleep

I

NARRATOR *(To audience.)* And meanwhile, gentlemen, we have reached the moment of inevitability: death.

(Enter FATHER OF WAITING MAN and MOTHER OF WALKING MAN.)

FATHER OF WAITING MAN: Which one of us?

NARRATOR: The old lady first.

MOTHER OF WALKING MAN: Where is he...I've been waiting...he was on his way to me...

NARRATOR: Yes, he almost came. He was on his way. He'll remember again at dawn, when he receives news of your death.

MOTHER OF WALKING MAN: He will come...he won't come... what does it matter? *(She falls.)* My former loved ones, I have already been through the little dramas of our lives, the love, the jealousy, the laughter, the dresses, even the constant worry for my only son, him with the suitcase at night, with his whole failed life – none of that interests me anymore. Now I'm just going from breath to breath. *(Starts wheezing again.)* If only you knew...if only you knew how difficult... it's indescribable... but then each of you will know one day... and now it is my turn... *(She stops wheezing, opens her eyes weakly.)* How's my condition? Coming around, I think...

NARRATOR: Yes, granny, getting better.

MOTHER OF WALKING MAN: *(Despondent, to herself.)* They're hiding something from me. *(To NARRATOR.)* Dampen my forehead…some moisture…

NARRATOR: There's no one to dampen it, granny, I've already told you, I'm not in the story, I'm just *telling* it. I can't help. You're completely on your own. *(MOTHER OF WALKING MAN sinks into unconsciousness. NARRATOR listens to her breathing.)* Expect the final breath.

FATHER OF WAITING MAN: *(Crying.)* If only I were healthy, and if only you were mine, I would run from room to room now with one great scream inside me: 'What a shame!' Everything we did not have time to do, the last trip we were planning to Lugano, the thing I want so urgently to tell you now, and so much else – What a shame! And I would run to you, I would cry and kiss your forehead and eyelids, and shout, 'Get up, woman whom I loved! What will I do without you?!'

(MOTHER OF WALKING MAN's wheezing dies out.)

NARRATOR: Dead. A person once dear to her mother has ceased to exist.

FATHER OF WAITING MAN: *(Through his tears; he regards the dead mother.)* While you were still dying, we could have, potentially, taken out a marriage license. That potential is gone. Because you have died and I am still alive. And dying as I may be, in that, I'm still ahead of you. For I am a man and a citizen, listed in the population registry, while you, at this moment, have been expunged from there, you cannot even bring to the marriage an identity card. That is why even potentially the matter is over and done with. Goodbye, matrimonial potential.

II

Enter TRIVIAL MAN and his mother.

MOTHER OF TRIVIAL MAN: *(To audience.)* Imagine death:
   imagine nothing, and then imagine even less. Imagine
   utter darkness and then imagine even greater darkness.
   Imagine what you cannot imagine, imagine everything
   you've known, the women, the rain, the bread rolls, the
   sun, then add to them the descriptive 'not.' Not-rain,
   not-sun, not-bread-rolls, not-women, imagine all that and
   erase imagination, too, because there are no more shapes,
   sounds, sensations, and do not be afraid, fear is erased,
   too, gone are the words – the negation words as well – and
   the word 'no' is erased, and the word ''not,' and noneness
   is gone, the nothing is multiplied, you cannot envision
   until you arrive, and when you arrive you'll envision no
   more.

NARRATOR: Tomorrow, you'll talk tomorrow. Come
   tomorrow.

MOTHER OF TRIVIAL MAN: Tomorrow.

   (TRIVIAL MAN and his mother exit.)

III

NARRATOR awakens MOTHER OF WALKING MAN.

MOTHER OF WALKING MAN: *(With suspicion.)* What's going
   on here? What is this place you've brought me to, here?

NARRATOR: Here is a very good place. Here you'll be very
   happy here.

MOTHER OF WALKING MAN: Is there a bit of water here?

NARRATOR: There's water flowing here perfectly fine here, too. *(He raises her up. Her dead parents enter.)* Here are your parents.

MOTHER OF WALKING MAN: Hello, Father, hello, Mother. I've come.

WALKING MAN'S MOTHER'S MOTHER: Who's the old lady?

NARRATOR: Your daughter.

WALKING MAN'S MOTHER'S MOTHER: That's the little girl with the dimples? *(To her daughter.)* Don't tell me what's happening out there and what you've been through. Lie down and be quiet.

MOTHER OF WALKING MAN: *(Laughs bitterly.)* And once again my parents, like they used to, have put me to bed. To lie down, to be quiet, to close my eyes. I've come home. *(She stands silently at their side.)*

WALKING MAN'S MOTHER'S FATHER: So-and-so.

WALKING MAN'S MOTHER'S MOTHER: So-and-so. Born so-and-so.

MOTHER OF WALKING MAN: So-and-so. Their daughter. From today. *(The dead people exit.)*

IV

WALKING MAN and WAITING MAN are walking. VAGUE THOUGHT and MURKY THOUGHT enter behind WALKING MAN.

VAGUE THOUGHT *(To MURKY THOUGHT.)* One day you will die. The memory of the kindergarten teacher and the pail will be gone. So will Ass and Pickled Herring; all of you, like foam on the water, will froth a moment then vanish, leaving only the clear, deep waters.

MURKY THOUGHT: One day *you* will die. There will be no more attempt to lift off, to find a single redemptive word, only shreds of simple memories, a pail, a kindergarten teacher, an ass, pickled herring, all these will hover a moment longer, like embers of an extinguished fire, aloft in the wind, they will fly, float and disappear.

(They exit. WALKING MAN and WAITING MAN continue walking.)

V

WALKING MAN and WAITING MAN are walking. They reach WAITING MAN's house.

WAITING MAN: I've come home. Here is my bed. I will lie down to sleep.

WALKING MAN: I liked the division into cantons. It felt good, like Switzerland.

WAITING MAN: And where is she, and when will she return, that's the question. That is the question, and there is no other. *(In a broken voice.)* What I would like more than anything is to stand before her with my hands in my pockets. She comes over and hugs me and I do not take my hands out, I just stand there whistling something. That is my dream.

WALKING MAN: Things will yet occur that have not been imagined.

WAITING MAN: I am waiting.

WALKING MAN: Prepare for the matter itself. For the time being, go to sleep and wait.

WAITING MAN: I am waiting. And you remember that our days are numbered. Life expectancy may be rising, but not enough.

WALKING MAN: Let us part. *(They shake hands. To himself.)* I will need a miracle.

WAITING MAN: *(To himself.)* I will expect salvation. *(WALKING MAN turns to leave, WAITING MAN sits on his bed, watching him go.)* Hey, and the chest? Left side…?

WALKING MAN: Thank you, thank you. *(He walks.)*

Act Seven: Putting Walking Man to Sleep

|

WALKING MAN continues walking. Behind him enter ASS THOUGHT, PICKLED HERRING THOUGHT, VAGUE THOUGHT, MURKY THOUGHT, arguing vehemently.

ASS THOUGHT: Forgive me, dear colleague…

PICKLED HERRING THOUGHT: *You* forgive *me*, learned idiot…

WALKING MAN: *(Turns to look at them.)* You again, you wandering thoughts, scattered shred by shred, aimless, without beginning or end…

PICKLED HERRING THOUGHT: But why be insulting, the ass served you well…

WALKING MAN: Can you not see how troubled I am now? How I long for the one pure thought. The me of long ago, the child I was: come draw me up from the bedrock of darkness!

(They try again while WALKING MAN covers his ears.)

ASS THOUGHT: I say…

PICKLED HERRING THOUGHT: I want….

MURKY THOUGHT: I remember…

VAGUE THOUGHT: If only…

(They give up and leave, shamefaced.)

(CHILD THOUGHT pops out from among the other THOUGHTS. WALKING MAN is at first stunned, and when he recognizes the child he smiles wearily.)

WALKING MAN: You? Were you walking behind me the whole way? *(CHILD THOUGHT stares at him wide-eyed and silent.)* But what do you want? I can do nothing for you. Understand, I don't even have the strength for myself. I cannot change your fate in any way. *(He continues walking, the child behind him. WALKING MAN runs off, the child in pursuit. WALKING MAN stops, suddenly grabs the child, and shakes him.)* But what? What do you want to tell me? What is trying to burst from that hole called your mouth? Which words are hiding in there? Something important? A revelation? Did you discover a magic potion that will redeem us all and you cannot articulate the formula? I look into your mouth and want to kiss it, to seal it with my lips and never remove them forevermore. *(He pushes the child away from himself. CHILD THOUGHT turns to leave. WALKING MAN calls after him.)* Hey! The 'me' of long ago! *(CHILD THOUGHT stops.)* Let me just trap the passing moment, here, like this, as you tilt your head slightly down and to the side, and the depths of heartbreaking despair are suddenly revealed in you, there, like that. I will remember you with that tilt of the head. I will remember the depths of despair. I will remember.

(CHILD THOUGHT exits.)

WALKING MAN reaches home, stops.

WALKING MAN: *(To himself.)* And finally, there is this strange matter of a step, and another, the space between two feet closes, this night walk is finished. Someone watching me through the window now will no longer call me the walking man. *(He stands facing the bed.)* Here is the bed. Here is the mattress. Here I will sit. I will be the sitting man. The still man. The man who exists for the time being. The man... how strange are words.

(Enter all THE THOUGHTS, all THE DYING and LIVING and DEAD, they all gather around him.)

NARRATOR *(To audience.)* And here they all are, all those who accompanied him this night.

FATHER OF WAITING MAN: *(Wheezing.)* How long do I have?

NARRATOR: Not long. *(Enter TRIVIAL MAN and his mother. Impatiently.)* You again! You've been told you're trivial here!

TRIVIAL MAN: And what are you? 'Trivial, trivial...' In the end they'll think I'm an uninteresting person. When's it my turn?

NARRATOR: Tomorrow, tomorrow is your story. Come tomorrow.

MOTHER OF TRIVIAL MAN: Tomorrow? So it'll be tomorrow. Same difference. *(Exit TRIVIAL MAN and his mother.)*

IV

SHY DEAD MAN bursts out crying. GOD enters and takes SHY DEAD MAN's face in his hands, trying to comfort him.

GOD: Shhhhh! *(SHY DEAD MAN stops crying.)* Nevertheless, there is something about you. Nevertheless, I loved you all. You were born, once upon a time, good, and gaping in endless wonder at the world, and you were so funny, and so vulnerable. I loved you all in your indignity. And if I do nothing for you, it is only because... *(The din of a passing train drowns out his words. It passes.)* ...and at least I will remember you favorably.

SHY DEAD MAN: And I would like to say... *(God stops. SHY DEAD MAN, cowed.)* And I would like to say something about dead people buried in the first rain of the season. *(Pause.)* They get good and wet. *(Pause.)* Mud. *(Pause.)* Despair. *(Pause. He is cowed, he does not know how to continue.)* That's all.

(GOD puts down his suitcase and sits on it as if very weak.)

SOUR DEAD WOMAN: Give God some water. God doesn't feel well.

NARRATOR: There's no faucet around here. It's night, everything's closed.

GOD: It's all right. A little better. *(He rises.)* I will remember, I will remember all of you favorably. *(To NARRATOR.)* And thanks to you for the storytelling effort.

NARRATOR: My pleasure, it really was an effort. *(God turns to leave.)* And what is it, your honor, that one feels on the left side of the chest?

GOD *(Stopping, turning on his heels.)* Rhyming pair: Little song.

NARRATOR: Bitty ditty.

GOD: Two points.

NARRATOR: And in the chest, the left side, when one breathes... *(But GOD has already exited and THE NARRATOR, with an awkward smile, waves goodbye and calls after him ingratiatingly.)* Nicely done, your honor...bitty ditty, eh? Bitty ditty... *(To himself, quietly.)* Bitty ditty and pretty kitty – and in the end, we'll die.

V

NARRATOR approaches WALKING MAN, who is sitting on his bed.

NARRATOR: So, you've tired yourself out. You're at your bed, a heavy fog in your brain.

WALKING MAN: Yes

NARRATOR: And you do not know that two blocks away your mother has died.

WALKING MAN: *(Tired and sad.)* No.

NARRATOR: And while she was dying, you were walking and laughing…

WALKING MAN: I wasn't laughing.

NARRATOR: But you were breathing. Admit it, you were breathing deeply while your mother was gasping for breath. And what's the point of walking? What's the point of trying to find cantons, playing at secret agents and gangs and huge brothels in Istanbul? What's the whole point when your mother died and you didn't even know?

WALKING MAN: *(Pleading, tears in his eyes.)* What can I do?

MOTHER OF WALKING MAN: *(Draws near WALKING MAN.)* So-and-so born so-and-so, I died on such-and-such a date in such-and-such a place. And such-and-such is the situation and thus it will continue. And between the walls of your skull, lit up by your imagination, my image will flicker a while longer, grow distant, blurry like all the world at day's end. I will be in you until I cease on the day of your death. Then we shall link arms and I will walk with you to the death that follows death – to oblivion.

(All THE LIVING, DEAD and DYING and THE THOUGHTS exit. WALKING MAN sits on his bed.)

238

NARRATOR *(Turning once again to WALKING MAN.)* But let us not get ahead of ourselves; for now, you still do not know of her death. For now, you're still busy with your little indecisions. Soon, with the first light of dawn, the neighbor will knock on your door to let you know. You will weep mightily with a small boy's wailing that you did not know existed in you. Over and done with are years of preparing for your mother's death.

WALKING MAN: It is no trifling matter, the death of my only mother. How foolish and ridiculous everything was in light of the bare, simple truth: My mother has died *(He cries.)* Mother, Mother…! *(Pressing on.)* But for the time being, I still know nothing.

NARRATOR *(To audience.)* Yes. There he sits, he does not know. Dawn rises. A knock at the door.

WALKING MAN: Enter! *(THE NEIGHBOR enters. WALKING MAN turns to him hesitantly, a seed of panic begins to sprout in him.)* What do you want at five in the morning? *(The messenger opens his mouth to speak, NARRATOR waves his hand to silence him.)*

NARRATOR: But that is a matter for another story. Ours has ended.

(WALKING MAN and NEIGHBOR freeze in place facing one another.)

END

REQUIEM

Translated by Lee Nishri-Howitt
and Leland Frankel

A tragedy based on three stories by Chekhov. An old village couple approaching the end of life; a coachman who has just lost his son and nobody wants to listen to his mourning; a young mother who refuses to cry over her dying baby; a group of drunkards and whores – all questioning the meaning of life, of suffering, of loneliness and unhappiness, with no answer in sight. A masterful *mélange* of storytelling and role-playing, one of Levin's most successful plays worldwide.

Cast of Characters

THE OLD MAN
THE OLD WOMAN
THE MOTHER
THE DRIVER
THE PROSTITUTE WITH A MOLE
THE PROSTITUTE WITH A FRECKLE
THE PUMPKIN-SHAPED DRUNK
THE ZUCCHINI-SHAPED DRUNK
THE MEDIC
THE HAPPY CHERUB
THE FUNNY CHERUB
THE SAD CHERUB

PRONUNCIATION GUIDE

'PUPKAH' : POOP-KUH

'KHLOPKA' : KLOPE-KUH
'SCHCHOCHI' : SH-CHO-CHI
'PJOJY' : PUH-JSHOH-JEE

'PUSHKALÉ' : PUSH-KUH-LAY
'PISHPUSHKALÉ' : PISH-PUSH-KUH-LAY

Premiere	The Cameri Theatre, Tel Aviv, 1998
Director	Hanoch Levin
Costume and Stage Design	Rakefet Levi
Light Design	Shai Yehuda'ee
Music composition	Yossi Ben-Nun
Musicians	Yossi Ben-Nun, Shmuel Elbaz, Shuki Volfus, Avner Yifat
Singer	Keren Hadar / Limor Oved / Yael Tzvi

Cast:

THE OLD MAN	Yossef Carmon
THE OLD WOMAN	Zaharira Harifai
THE DRIVER	Yitshak Hizkia
PROSTITUTE WITH A MOLE	Florence Bloch
PROSTITUTE WITH A FRECKLE	Sigalit Fuchs
THE MEDIC	Shabtai Conorti
THE PUMPKINSHAPED DRUNK	Gabi Amrani
THE ZUCCHINISHAPED DRUNK	Shimon Mimran
THE HAPPY CHERUB	Dror Keren
THE FUNNY CHERUB	Alon Noiman
THE SAD CHERUB	Dina Blei
THE MOTHER	Sandra Schonwald
THE SHADOW PEOPLE	Simon Krichli, Yossi Rachmani, Roman Krichli, Shai Feinberg, Tal Ben-Bina, Shani Treisman
SINGER	Keren Hadar

SCENE 1

A cabin. Evening. In the cabin, an OLD MAN and OLD WOMAN.

OLD MAN: Our little town, Pupkah, was worse than a village.
Only a few old people still lived there, and they'd die so
rarely – the cheap bastards – that it could drive you crazy.
We had no wars and no real plagues to speak of; it's as
if everybody was holding on to their lives out of spite.
Anyway, bad news when you build coffins for a living. If
I made coffins in the city, folks would've called me 'Sir,'
but here in Pupkah – We live in poverty, in an old one
room cabin myself, the old woman, an oven, a bed, and
the coffins.

(THE OLD WOMAN is busy doing housework.)

You'd never say to yourself: Something worthwhile is
about to happen to this woman.

(THE OLD WOMAN keeps at it, breathing hard.)

Woman, why are you wheezing? You've cleaned up
quietly for fifty years, and all of a sudden it's…

(He makes wheezing sounds.)

You're making me deaf.

(Pause.)

What's wrong with you, woman?

OLD WOMAN: Can barely breathe…

OLD MAN: So you have a cold. It'll pass.

OLD WOMAN: Dizzy…Legs are shaking…

OLD MAN: You have a cold! The flu.

OLD WOMAN: …thirsty all day…

OLD MAN: But you stoked the fire this morning, like always.

OLD WOMAN: I did.

OLD MAN: You even brought water from the well.

OLD WOMAN: I did.

OLD MAN: It'll pass. Would you stop it with the wheezing already? I'm trying to count.

(Pause. THE OLD WOMAN keeps working. She doesn't speak and soon starts wheezing again.)

I still hear wheezing.

OLD WOMAN: What can I do…can barely…

(Pause. THE OLD WOMAN continues tidying up the room and then gets into bed. THE OLD MAN sits next to the table, yawns, and keeps balancing his ledger. Night. Silence.)

OLD MAN: *(Abruptly, to THE OLD WOMAN.)* Oh, these losses. Our chief of police was deathly ill for two years, dying, and then all of sudden he goes to Pjojy, the provincial capital, to get better. Boom! Just like that he dies and gets buried over there! Slipped right out of my fingers, what a mess! And what a coffin they must have ordered for him! But he had to drop dead somewhere else and screw me over! An entire month's pay, one hundred rubles, right out the window! And if I calculate annually… *(Calculates intensely.)* then it's…twelve hundred!

(Appalled, he shouts again.)

Twelve hundred rubles!

(THE OLD WOMAN jolts up in bed, frightened.)

OLD WOMAN: What's wrong?!

OLD MAN: I lost twelve hundred rubles in one year! And if I'd deposited those twelve hundred – that could've been an extra forty! Everywhere you turn, nothing but losses and more losses.

(Wheezes and chirps come out of her throat, and then suddenly –)

OLD WOMAN: Husband! I'm dying.

(THE OLD MAN looks at her, as if seeing her for the first time.)

My face was ablaze from the fever, but it was bright and joyful. You, who were used to seeing it forever pale, so scared and pitiful, you were sitting awkwardly across from me. It was evident that though I was indeed dying, I was happy to finally leave this cabin, these coffins, and you. I looked at the ceiling, puckered my lips, and my expression was joyous! As if I saw Death as my saving angel, and here I was whispering with him.

(Pause.)

I'm thirsty…water…

(He brings her water and supports her as she drinks.)

OLD MAN: And then for some reason I remembered that all through our lives, I have never caressed you.

Not even once have I felt sorry for you. Fifty-two years we've been together, long, long years…How is it that all of that time I haven't thought of you once, haven't noticed you? Like you were a dog or a cat? Every day you stoked this fire, cooked, baked, drew water from the well, chopped wood, and slept in my bed; Each time I came home drunk you would fold my pants with such respect. And me? It never crossed my mind to buy you a scarf or bring you a piece of candy; I wouldn't even let you drink tea, just to save a few rubles. So you'd meekly settle for hot water instead. Now I realize why your face is so strangely joyful and I am struck with fear.

(Pause.)

I'll make you tea, woman.

(THE OLD WOMAN shakes her head.)

Tea will make it better.

(Again, THE OLD WOMAN shakes her head.)

Come, woman, we'll go to the medic in Khlopka.

(He sighs.)

Another expense.

SCENE 2

The main road. Night. THE OLD MAN and OLD WOMAN.

OLD MAN: We stood on the road that night waiting for the troika. The voices of jackals from afar, frogs in the swamp, crickets chirping…as if they were all cheering: 'No matter what happens to *you*, here life goes on!'

(Pause. Then, to THE OLD WOMAN –)

Well, say something.

OLD WOMAN: *(With a creaky voice.)* What…

OLD MAN: Do you know where we're going?

OLD WOMAN: I know…We're going to Momma and Poppa.

OLD MAN: What do you mean, 'Momma and Poppa?'

OLD WOMAN: My Momma and Poppa.

OLD MAN: Your mother and father, may they rest in peace, have been dead for thirty years. We're going to the medic in Khlopka. He'll make you better.

(Pause.)

Well?

OLD WOMAN: What?

OLD MAN: Do you know where we're going?

OLD WOMAN: I do. We're going to Momma and Poppa.

OLD MAN: *(Distressed.)* Woman, what's with you? Do me a favor, pull yourself together.

(Pause.)

Soon the troika will arrive and we'll go.

OLD WOMAN: To Momma and Poppa.

OLD MAN: Why not? Momma and Poppa will be there too, eventually.

(Pause.)

Then we heard the rattle of the wheels, the squeak of the bearings, the hoofbeats drawing near.

(The troika arrives. In it are a DRIVER and two PROSTITUTES.)

OLD MAN: Is this the troika from Pjojy to Schchochi?

DRIVER: It is. Are you headed to Schchochi?

OLD MAN: No, sir. Not that far. We're from here. From Pupkah. We're going to see the medic in Khlopka. The old woman's sick.

DRIVER: Get in.

PROSTITUTE WITH A MOLE: *(To THE PROSTITUTE WITH A FRECKLE.)* Me, I like to eat pickled herring after a job. So what?

PROSTITUTE WITH A FRECKLE: But what if you've got another one right after?

PROSTITUTE WITH A MOLE: So there's another one. So what? Let him smell it. Where does it say that I gotta starve myself? Anyway, I'm not selling my mouth, just my *pushkalé.* He can stick his *pishpushkalé* in the *pushkalé* and be grateful. They don't wanna, they don't hafta. Let him plug his nose.

(THE DRIVER, trying not to laugh, winks at THE OLD MAN.)

DRIVER: Ha ha! Jolly ladies!

PROSTITUTE WITH A FRECKLE: Say what you will, that's not how they do it in Paris. In Paris you have to smell like perfume. Even your mouth. It's part of the job. But here in Pjojy nobody takes care of themselves. They've got no respect for their 'Divine Image.' The East might be falling apart, but out West they're more evolved. Everything is state of the art. Why we're dragging our tired bones to Schchochi, I have no idea.

PROSTITUTE WITH A MOLE: I heard that Schchochi is more like Paris.

PROSTITUTE WITH A FRECKLE: I wish. A new life…Maybe we'll finally meet that billionaire, Gazpacho De Bello! If he happens to be travelling from Paris to Shanghai, or Shanghai to Paris, he has to go through Pjojy and Schchochi!

DRIVER: And me? My son died a week ago.

PROSTITUTE WITH A MOLE: What are you blabbing about your son?

250

DRIVER: He died a week ago. Got sick all of a sudden.

PROSTITUTE WITH A FRECKLE: Yeah, everybody gets sick around here. They get sick in Paris too, but not as much. It's mostly due to hygiene.

PROSTITUTE WITH A MOLE: I actually wash out my *pushkalé* after every job.

PROSTITUTE WITH A FRECKLE: Yeah, but you're washing with water.

PROSTITUTE WITH A MOLE: So what? What should I wash it with?

PROSTITUTE WITH A FRECKLE: You have to disinfect, you idiot!

PROSTITUTE WITH A MOLE: Next you're gonna say, 'In Paris they disinfect!'

PROSTITUTE WITH A FRECKLE: What do you think? Of course they do!

PROSTITUTE WITH A MOLE: How long can you go, 'In Paris! In Paris!' Have you ever even been to Paris?

PROSTITUTE WITH A FRECKLE: I read about it.

PROSTITUTE WITH A MOLE: No you didn't.

PROSTITUTE WITH A FRECKLE: I skimmed.

PROSTITUTE WITH A MOLE: Skimmed what? You've never bought a magazine!

PROSTITUTE WITH A FRECKLE: I once bought some pickled herring, and it was wrapped in a page from a French magazine. I smoothed out the paper and there was a picture of a beautiful French woman from Paris!

PROSTITUTE WITH A MOLE: *(Laughing.)* And what did that idiot get? All her perfume, and she still winds up wrapped around a fish!

DRIVER: And me? My son died a week ago, my only son...

PROSTITUTE WITH A MOLE: *(Bursting out laughing.)* Wrapped around a fish!

(Both PROSTITUTES laugh.)

DRIVER: Jolly ladies! What a life! And here we are in Khlopka.

(THE OLD MAN and THE OLD WOMAN get off. The troika departs.)

SCENE 3

Cabin. Night. THE MEDIC is asleep in his bed, snoring. Enter THE OLD MAN and OLD WOMAN.

OLD MAN: We stood at the entrance of the medic's cabin in the town of Khlopka, which looked just like our own cabin in Pupkah, only instead of coffins there were a few jars; and instead of an old woman, a goat.

(To THE OLD WOMAN:)

Woman, don't be upset we're only seeing the medic. You oughta be glad; they say this man, even though he's a real drunk, and sometimes hits his own patients, knows more about medicine than any great doctor.

(They both approach THE MEDIC.)

Hello, Mister Doctor.

(THE MEDIC keeps sleeping. THE OLD MAN yells:)

Hello, Mister Doctor!

(He shakes THE MEDIC.)

Hello, Mister Doctor!

(THE MEDIC wakes up and shivers.)

MEDIC: What doctor?

OLD MAN: Oh, *more* than a doctor! Greetings! Sorry to bother you with our petty troubles, but as you can see, my wife here, my wife of many years, is…how do you say…sick. With respect.

(THE MEDIC cuts him off with a wave. He gestures for THE OLD WOMAN to sit on the bed. She takes a seat, listless. Her mouth is open and she breathes heavily. THE MEDIC looks at her. Pause.)

MEDIC: Mmm…Yeah…Uh-huh…

(Pause.)

The flu, or maybe a fever. There's been an outbreak of typhus in the city.

OLD MAN: Typhus? We had no idea.

MEDIC: Yeaaaaah…Well, so what? The woman lived, thank God. How old is she?

OLD MAN: Not even seventy! Sixty-nine!

MEDIC: Sixty-nine, well, what do you want? She bloomed, and soon she'll be picked.

OLD MAN: True, Mister Doctor…*More* than a doctor. You make a good point…I mean…and thank you for your patience, and for receiving us so pleasantly. But you understand, even a fly or a flea wants to live.

MEDIC: So they wanna live. So what? Put a cold compress on her head and give her these powders twice a day. *Buonasera.*

OLD MAN: Before or after she eats?

MEDIC: Doesn't matter. *Buonasera.*

(He lies down on his bed and closes his eyes.)

OLD MAN: From the look on his face I knew that
circumstances were dire, and that no compress or powder
would be of any use. Now it became clear to me that
my old woman would be dead soon; if not today, then
tomorrow.

(He shakes THE MEDIC quietly and whispers:)

Mister Doctor, maybe we should bleed her.

MEDIC: There's no time, my friend, no time. I've got people
waiting. Take your old woman and goodbye. *Buonasera.*

OLD MAN: Do us this kindness, please, for your honor knows
that if this were a matter of the stomach, or the guts or
intestines, that's when you would prescribe powders and
drops. But this is a matter of a cold, so first you have to bleed!

MEDIC: Out! Out! Stop pestering me!

OLD MAN: At least apply leeches! For the rest of my days I
will pray for your health!

MEDIC: Well! Still standing there and running off at the
mouth! What a blockhead!

(THE MEDIC falls asleep.)

OLD MAN: So in Khlopka they spare leeches, but not old
women! Come, let's go home.

(He leaves with THE OLD WOMAN.)

SCENE 4

The main road. Dawn. THE OLD MAN and OLD WOMAN.

OLD MAN: At dawn we stood on the main road outside of
Khlopka and waited for the troika to return. It was a
beautiful, intoxicating spring morning. The birds were
chirping wildly, with gusto. All of nature seemed to be
leaping towards a new day, and it felt like everything had
a purpose, unknown though it may be.

(THE OLD WOMAN wheezes.)

You'll get better, woman. You'll get better. You've been
well for sixty-nine years. No reason to stop now.

*(Enter the troika, THE DRIVER, and two DRUNKS. THE OLD MAN
and OLD WOMAN get in.)*

DRIVER: So, Grandpa, did it do any good?

OLD MAN: None. But she'll get better on her own.

DRIVER: Mm. My son died a week ago. I took him to the
hospital, too…

ZUCCHINI-SHAPED DRUNK: Go, go already! Don't just stand
here all day!

DRIVER: I'm going, sir, I'm going.

*(The troika pulls away and the two DRUNKS continue their
interrupted conversation.)*

ZUCCHINI-SHAPED DRUNK: Anyway, they both smelled like
pickled herring! Disgusting!

PUMPKIN-SHAPED DRUNK: Mine wouldn't stop talking about
some Gazpacho or Carpaccio…*Something* De Bello. But
what did you expect from Schchochi? They say in Pjojy,
the females are more…

(To THE DRIVER:)

Hey! Any good broads in Pjojy?

DRIVER: Oh, jolly fellows! Ha ha! In Pjojy, in Schchochi... where *aren't* there?

ZUCCHINI-SHAPED DRUNK: But good ones! Good ones! That don't smell, for Godsakes! 'Cause here, sure, everything is burning to the ground, but we've still got standards. And not too pricey. And gorgeous! Are they gorgeous in Pjojy? And not greedy. I don't like 'em greedy! I like 'em generous. Ones that don't do it for the money, but to serve a higher purpose! And not only that – they also give it up for free because it's their birthday, or Independence Day, or Philanthropy Day or something. Who live alone in a big house!

PUMPKIN-SHAPED DRUNK: And there's a big sign over the door that says...'Tswidan.'

DRIVER: Ha ha!

PUMPKIN-SHAPED DRUNK: I bet you're wondering, 'What's 'Tswidan'?'

DRIVER: Why wonder? You see, my son...

PUMPKIN-SHAPED DRUNK: I bet you're thinking, 'It's some venereal disease or the name of a famous pirate!'

DRIVER: Ha ha! Jolly masters!

PUMPKIN-SHAPED DRUNK: So why aren't you asking, 'What's that 'Tswidan' hanging over the door?'

DRIVER: Ha ha! What is Tswidan?

PUMPKIN-SHAPED DRUNK: It stands for This Slut Wants It Day And Night!

(He laughs.)

DRIVER: Ha ha!

ZUCCHINI-SHAPED DRUNK: *(With a sour expression.)* Why 'Tswidan?' It should be Tswidanaadth: 'This Slut Wants It Day And Night And Also During The Holidays!'

(THE PUMPKIN-SHAPED DRUNK laughs harder.)

ZUCCHINI-SHAPED DRUNK: Tswidanaadthaaff!

DRIVER: Ha ha!

ZUCCHINI-SHAPED DRUNK: 'This Slut Wants It Day And Night And Also During The Holidays And All For Free!'

DRIVER: Ha ha!

ZUCCHINI-SHAPED DRUNK: Tswidanaadthaaffagybscew! 'This Slut Wants It Day And Night And Also During The Holidays And All For Free And Gives You Back Small Change Either Way!'

PUMPKIN-SHAPED DRUNK: *(Sing-song.)* 'On the planet of Tswidanaadthaaffagybscew/I shake my little thingie 'til it turns all blue!'

DRIVER: We've reached Pupkah.

(THE OLD MAN and OLD WOMAN get off. The troika keeps going.)

SCENE 5

(Cabin. Morning. THE OLD MAN and OLD WOMAN. She stands, leaning against the wall.)

OLD WOMAN: After we returned home and entered our cabin, I stood for about ten minutes just leaning against the oven. It seemed to me then that if I lay down, you would start talking about losses again, and curse me for resting when I ought to be working.

OLD MAN: And I looked at you with astonishment, and remembered that tomorrow is a holiday, and the day after that, too. And then the day after *that* is a Saturday, which meant that I was forbidden from working for three whole days, three days during which you would undoubtedly die. And so your coffin had to be built today.

(He lays her down.)

OLD MAN: So I grabbed the ruler and took your measurements.

(He grabs the ruler and measures her, then goes to the table and writes in his ledger.)

OLD MAN: 'For my wife: One coffin. Two…and a half rubles.' Do I count this as an expense, or a profit?

OLD WOMAN: And I lay in silence with my eyes closed until evening came.

(Night falls.)

OLD WOMAN: When it got darker, I suddenly cried out: Husband! Do you remember, do you remember how fifty years ago God gave us a little baby girl? She was born with such golden curls. Do you remember how we both sat there on the riverbank and sang her songs beneath the willow tree?

(She lets out a cry of grief.)

OLD WOMAN: She died after a week!

OLD MAN: A baby girl? A willow tree? What kind of delusion is that?

OLD WOMAN: And so I looked at the wall, turning my back to this world.

(She takes her last breaths. THE OLD MAN leans over her and suddenly says, with a choked voice–)

OLD MAN: Don't leave me!

OLD WOMAN: And the instant before I died I fell asleep. How odd for a person to sleep right before the Greatest Sleep Of All. But so it was. I fell asleep, and just for a moment I dreamed: We were at our house, in the afternoon. My mother and father were laughing about something. I wasn't sure what about, but this I knew for certain – It was a rare opportunity. For a moment my parents had forgotten how bad things were, and so I quickly joined their laughter. Oh, how they laughed! And I looked up at them with the eyes of a child and I laughed – not knowing why – even harder than they did. Then all at once their laughter stopped. But I tried to keep laughing, just a little longer. I wanted the laughter to go on and on. I knew that as long as you laugh, all is well. There is no hurt and no hunger and no worry. But the laughter stopped, and after a few attempts I stopped as well. The house went silent, and it grew dark. Perhaps the day got darker, or perhaps I did.

(Three CHERUBS enter.)

HAPPY CHERUB: It was the day! The day got darker, not you!

FUNNY CHERUB: And you can keep laughing! With us, you can keep laughing, and laughing…

HAPPY CHERUB: Shall we tickle you?

FUNNY CHERUB: Tickletickletickletickletickle?

SAD CHERUB: Her flesh can no longer be tickled.

HAPPY CHERUB: Do you feel like crying?

FUNNY CHERUB: Where does it hurt?

HAPPY CHERUB: Show us!

FUNNY CHERUB: Where does it hurt? Shall we kiss the pain away?

(The CHERUBS kiss her.)

OLD WOMAN: Right here…No, there. It hurts there…No, here.

(Pause.)

And I passed from that small, dreamful sleep into the Great one, of which I cannot say a thing.

(She dies. The CHERUBS exit.)

SCENE 6

The riverbank. Morning. THE OLD MAN.

OLD MAN: After I left that small cemetery, I didn't go back home. Instead, I just followed my feet wherever they lead me, all the way to the pasture. Some children were there. Further along, at the edge of town, was the river. Crows were shrieking, ducks were splashing, the sun burned hot, and the water gleamed so brightly that it hurt my eyes. I walked along the bank, and the children cried out after me: 'Coffin maker!' But I kept walking, until I reached an ancient willow tree with a gnarled trunk. And suddenly, I recalled with extraordinary clarity a golden-haired baby and a willow tree of old! These are the ones you'd spoken of! Yes, this is that same willow tree. Green, quiet, sad… My, how you've aged!

(He sits down.)

And I wonder…I can't understand how, for the last fifty years, I've never come here even once. Beyond the cabin, beyond the coffins, just outside our window was this great, extraordinary world! And I had no inkling of it. This is a real river too, not some petty stream! I could have started a fishing business here. And the fish I could have sold on the shore, at the restaurant I might have opened for the tourists! And I could have put those profits in the bank, and gained interest on them! It would have been better than coffins! And the geese I could have hunted, and fattened up and slaughtered, and then sent their feathers down the river for making pillows in the big city! And if we put it all together, the coffins, the fish, the geese, the pillows…Why, we would've made a fortune! What losses! Oh, what a waste! My life has passed by without profit or pleasure. I've left behind nothing but losses! And they are so terrible! So chillingly terrible! Why did they chop down the woods on the other bank? Why are there no sheep in the pasture? Why did I not take pity on my wife, not even once in my entire life?

(THE MOTHER enters, carrying a baby wrapped in a blanket.)

MOTHER: Hello.

(THE OLD MAN doesn't respond.)

Schchochi, is it still very far?

(THE OLD MAN still doesn't respond.)

I'm from the next town, Drupka. I'm headed to the hospital in Schchochi with my baby.

OLD MAN: The road is long. You'll have to ride.

MOTHER: I don't have any money.

(She gestures towards the baby as THE OLD MAN stands still.)

MOTHER: He's quiet because he's asleep. She poured a
bucket of boiling water on him, because she was mad
about the inheritance. We were in the laundry room. I was
doing the laundry, and he lay there looking at the ceiling.
Only six months old. She took a bucket of boiling water
and poured it over him, just like that. He screamed for
maybe an hour, then fell asleep. Took a bucket of boiling
water and poured. Now he's asleep. Why can't I wake
him up?

OLD MAN: You won't make it to Schchochi on foot. There's a
medic in Khlopka.

MOTHER: This is my only child. I'm not even seventeen yet.

(She exits.)

SCENE 7

(A road in the fields. Day. THE MOTHER walks with the baby in her arms.)

MOTHER: I walked and walked all day. My brain was empty.
I couldn't think of anything. I just let my feet walk. It
was good to walk like that. When you walk, you feel that
things are going to turn out for the best. At sundown I
reached the medic's cabin in the town of Khlopka.

SCENE 8

(Cabin. Evening. THE MEDIC sits and smokes. THE MOTHER walks in, the baby in her arms.)

MOTHER: Hello.

(Pause.)

Hello there, Mister Medic, sir. I'm from the town of
Drupka. I came here with my baby. She poured a bucket

of boiling water over him. We were in the laundry room.
I was doing the laundry and he lay there looking at the
ceiling. Only six months old. Took a bucket of boiling
water and poured. At first he screamed for maybe an hour
and then he fell asleep. He's been asleep ever since, Mister
Medic, and I can't wake him up. Here, look. I can't.

(THE MEDIC looks at the baby.)

MEDIC: Yeaaaaah…

MOTHER: Why can't I wake him up? Isn't he hungry? He
always wakes up every three or four hours to eat, but
now…

MEDIC: Yeaaaaah…

(He prods the baby. Pause.)

MOTHER: Make him live, sir.

(Pause.)

Just make him live.

MEDIC: Pray.

MOTHER: I do pray. I've been praying all day. It's my only
child, my first and only. Why would somebody pour
boiling water over a six month old baby who's lying there
and smiling at the ceiling?

MEDIC: Here. Wrap him in a cold compress, and wait over
there next to that fence.

*(THE MOTHER goes aside with the baby and wraps him in bandages.
Enter the three CHERUBS.)*

HAPPY CHERUB: *(Leaning over the unconscious baby.)* Shall I tell
you a story?

(Pause.)

Once upon a time, there was a boy. He was the son of
a king, but nobody knew it except for him. How sad he
was that all the princesses in the world would walk by his
window without a second glance. He lay there in his bed
and wouldn't eat anything. He got thinner and thinner
every day. Eventually, he got really sick. He couldn't
move, just lay there with his eyes open, and waited. One
night, when the moon shone brightly, a beautiful princess
passed by and, finally, stopped at his window and looked
in. Through the fog of her breath, the dust, the dirt,
through her own reflection, she saw him. He was too weak
to talk. Tears rolled down his cheeks.

(Pause.)

Would you rather hear the story with the hat?

(He puts a hat on his head.)

Once upon a time, there was a boy. He was the son of
a king, but nobody knew it except for him. How sad he
was that all the princesses in the world would walk by his
window without a second glance. He lay there in his bed
and wouldn't eat anything. He got thinner and thinner
every day. Eventually, he got really sick. He couldn't
move, just lay there with his eyes open, and waited. One
night, when the moon shone brightly, a beautiful princess
passed by and, finally, stopped at his window and looked
in. Through the fog of her breath, the dust, the dirt,
through her own reflection, she saw him. He was too weak
to talk. Tears rolled down his cheeks.

(Pause.)

Should I tell you the story with the two hats?

(He puts another hat on his head.)

Once upon a time…He stopped breathing.

FUNNY CHERUB: Is that in the story?

SAD CHERUB: That's in a different story.

(The three CHERUBS exit. THE MOTHER wraps the baby, picks him up, and leaves.)

SCENE 9

(A road in the fields. Night. THE MOTHER walks with the dead baby in her arms.)

MOTHER: I hurried back. Somewhere on the way I lost my shawl. I looked up at the sky and wondered: Where is my baby's soul now? Is it following me? Or is it carried up there amongst the stars and doesn't even think of me anymore? How lonely it is in this field at night amongst this song of nature. Surrounded by the sounds of joy, when I myself can neither sing nor be cheerful; when a moon hangs up above, as lonely as I am. He doesn't care if it's spring now or winter, if people live or if they die.

SCENE 10

(The riverbank. Morning. THE OLD MAN is seated next to the willow tree. Enter THE MOTHER with the dead baby in her arms. THE OLD MAN stands up and approaches her.)

OLD MAN: Hello there.

MOTHER: Hello.

OLD MAN: You're back.

MOTHER: He died.

OLD MAN: *(Looking at the dead baby.)* He's so small. Our little girl was even smaller...

MOTHER: He squirmed around a little longer, then he died.

OLD MAN: Where are you taking him?

(Pause.)

You should bury him here on the riverbank beneath that willow tree.

(Pause.)

I'll make a coffin for him.

MOTHER: I don't have any money.

OLD MAN: Nobody has money these days. They're all...I'm a carpenter. I make coffins.

MOTHER: I'll bury him in the ground as he is.

OLD MAN: You'd only need about two feet of wood. It's a small matter, not much bigger than a shoebox.

MOTHER: No. I'll bury him like this, with nothing between his body and nature.

OLD MAN: I can make you some tea. You'll be warmer.

MOTHER: Are you a saint?

OLD MAN: No. I'm from Pupkah.

MOTHER: You must be a saint.

OLD MAN: Oh, what a saint am I.

(He weeps briefly and then ceases.)

At least let me help you bury h-

MOTHER: I'll do it by myself. By myself.

(She digs a hole and puts the baby in it.)

You were still silent and so small...Words had not yet been given to you for your pain. You had only ever wept a handful of times. You cried a little when you were hungry. You cried when you gazed up at the sky and saw what sort of world you had come into. And then one more enormous, prolonged cry came out when they poured the boiling water on you and something within you knew: This life, short and bleak, was over.

(She covers the hole and kneels next to it. THE OLD MAN starts walking away, but then stops and turns towards her.)

OLD MAN: If you desperately need a saint, then I am a saint. Speak to me.

(She says nothing. He approaches her.)

You have been wronged.

MOTHER: Yes, sir.

OLD MAN: And you, what did you do after she poured the boiling water on him?

MOTHER: Nothing, sir.

OLD MAN: And you did nothing beforehand?

MOTHER: No, sir.

OLD MAN: And what have you done with your life, my child?

MOTHER: I did the laundry. I swept the floors.

OLD MAN: But what greater deeds have you performed?

MOTHER: I didn't, sir.

OLD MAN: You were a person. You have a brain, your own will. What have you done with those?

MOTHER: I lived, sir.

OLD MAN: Have you never stood at a crossroads?

MOTHER: No, sir.

OLD MAN: Have you never said, 'I'll go this way, and that way I won't?'

MOTHER: No, sir. Life lead the way and I followed.

OLD MAN: What a life, my child!

MOTHER: It's just the way everybody lives, sir. I stood in line to get my pinch of sugar. But the line was long and my turn never came.

OLD MAN: And *we* didn't see all these years that there was a river and a willow tree and that once a little girl with golden curls had been born.

(Pause.)

Now you kneel in front of me and offer your face for me to touch and console you. But well you know that I am just as miserable as yourself and that my touch brings neither blessing nor solace.

MOTHER: Do as you see fit, sir.

(THE OLD MAN stands in front of her for a moment, unsure of what to do. He touches her cheek.)

OLD MAN: Here, I'll hold your head so you can cry a little.

(Pause. She is silent.)

If you cried it would be easier for you.

(Pause.)

MOTHER: If I cried, sir, it would have been easier for the world. They would say, 'There is wrong, but there is also release.' I will not cry. And if they ask me, 'Have you never stood at a crossroads?' I'll answer, 'I have. One evening over the grave of my baby. I could have cried or kept silent. And I made my decision.'

OLD MAN: So...So it is. Just like that.

(He walks away. Pause. THE MOTHER breaks out sobbing and prostrates herself over the grave. She forcibly swallows down her cries as she speaks.)

MOTHER: My baby! My baby! Here, I'll close my eyes. I'll see bushes and leaves. Here they are, full of color, in bloom. And I say: Here are the leaves. Life. Everything is in bloom. And amongst the leaves are my father and mother, my uncles and aunts, and there you are as well. Here you are! My baby, you are there, you're alive, and who says hallucinations are lies? Our life is a lie. The world is a lie. The real world is created when we close our eyes. Reality is there when we open them no longer.

(Enter the three CHERUBS. THE MOTHER turns her head to them with closed eyes.)

What do you say, cherubs? Should I open my eyes or keep them shut?

HAPPY CHERUB: Open them.

FUNNY CHERUB: But also keep them closed.

HAPPY CHERUB: Let there be no eyelids.

FUNNY CHERUB: Instead of eyelids, let there be a screen.

HAPPY CHERUB: And it'll go up...

FUNNY CHERUB: ...and behind it there'll be a light...

HAPPY CHERUB: ...a light that will reveal everything...

FUNNY CHERUB: ...but will also blind you.

HAPPY CHERUB: And behind the light there will be a bell...

FUNNY CHERUB: …that will ring loudly.

HAPPY CHERUB: And you can hear it so…

FUNNY CHERUB: …that you can't hear it at all.

SAD CHERUB: Enough. You can't laugh all day.

MOTHER: Why not? Laugh away. My baby laughed once. He was lying on his back and saw a fly on the ceiling, and all of a sudden he laughed his heart out, as if saying to himself: 'What is that, that fly? How funny it is that things…'

SAD CHERUB: And now you have a note from him. From your baby.

(He takes out a piece of paper and shows it to her.)

He can't write or speak, so we translated.

(He reads from the piece of paper:)

'Mommy, I'm asleep. A deep sleep with no dreams. Yesterday I fell asleep and I won't wake up anymore. Why would I? No more fear, pain, or worry. And my smile, little by little with the years, will only grow bigger.'

(The three CHERUBS exit. THE OLD MAN, from a distance, says quietly with his eyes closed:)

OLD MAN: My little girl, where are you buried? Where are you, my golden-curled child?

MOTHER: And then I opened my eyes. The night grew darker. Stars were shining in the distance. Nobody passed by. I stood up and left.

(She exits.)

SCENE 11

(The main road. Twilight. THE OLD MAN.)

OLD MAN: And then I felt this dryness in my mouth. My head was feverish and my feet were heavy. Once again I stood and waited where I had before with the old woman. The sun had set and the night grew darker. And then I heard the rattling of wheels and the squeak of the bearings. There it was, the same troika, the same driver.

(The troika arrives with a DRIVER and two DRUNKS. It stops.)

DRIVER: To Schchochi?

OLD MAN: To the medic in Khlopka. I rode with you a week ago with my wife.

DRIVER: Who can remember?

OLD MAN: Now I am sick too.

DRIVER: And me? Two weeks ago my son –

OLD MAN: So now I am taking myself to the medic in Khlopka.

(He struggles to get into the troika. The two DRUNKS continue their interrupted conversation.)

PUMPKIN-SHAPED DRUNK: But they say that in Pjojy, they don't smell as bad. They're classier.

ZUCCHINI-SHAPED DRUNK: *(Fuming.)* But we just came from Pjojy!

PUMPKIN-SHAPED DRUNK: Sorry, I meant in Schchochi.

ZUCCHINI-SHAPED DRUNK: Before that we were in Schchochi! We were in Schchochi, we went to Pjojy, and now we're back in Schchochi! And even there they go on and on about this Gazpacho or Carpaccio De Bello! What's their deal with this De Bello? And the smell!

PUMPKIN-SHAPED DRUNK: That's the problem with these nether regions we desire so: Always stuffy, stinky, and sweaty. Even the French ones!

ZUCCHINI-SHAPED DRUNK: Oh, you and your French women. You ever even nailed a French one?

PUMPKIN-SHAPED DRUNK: Oh boy, have I my friend. I've nailed 'em all.

ZUCCHINI-SHAPED DRUNK: They reek and then they die, huh?

PUMPKIN-SHAPED DRUNK: Of course! People think: There you have it – An elegant oval dining room in a French castle, full of furniture and fine china. And at the head of the table sits a beautiful French woman and they think: Surely it must be so. This is ordained by nature. From the beginning of time, the universe has demanded it. But if you were to blow it all up, the French woman, the oval dining room, the whole castle, only a void would be left behind. And there is no universal necessity for any French woman.

ZUCCHINI-SHAPED DRUNK: *(Bursts out laughing.)* She sits there at the end of the table like she was eternal, and she still gets blown up!

DRIVER: *(Trying to join in on the laughter.)* Jolly fellows! The world goes round!

PUMPKIN-SHAPED DRUNK: *(Laughing along.)* And when they blow up and disappear, everyone is surprised and goes: 'Oh!'

(He bursts out laughing again.)

THEY GO: 'Oh!'

(Laughing harder.)

'Oh!'

ZUCCHINI-SHAPED DRUNK: *(Stops laughing, with a sour expression.)* You may have nailed French women, but 'complex thought' is not your forte. Not so much 'depth,' either.

DRIVER: Well, my son died two weeks ago. Got sick all of a sudden.

PUMPKIN-SHAPED DRUNK: What? What happened there, my little friend? A tragedy? Tragedies happen. Always have, always will.

DRIVER: But only two weeks ago…

(THE PUMPKIN-SHAPED DRUNK falls asleep. He snores.)

ZUCCHINI-SHAPED DRUNK: What happened two weeks ago?

DRIVER: I had…and he died…

ZUCCHINI-SHAPED DRUNK: What?

DRIVER: Never mind.

ZUCCHINI-SHAPED DRUNK: *(Sourly yawning.)* Oh, what a calamity! When do we retire our desires? Best thing is just to be an old English lady with a cat.

(His head rolls sideways and he falls asleep. THE DRIVER turns to THE OLD MAN.)

DRIVER: He was healthy. He drove the troika. He was my only son and then suddenly…

OLD MAN: I'm sick.

DRIVER: *(With a sigh.)* Yes.

(Pause.)

We've reached Khlopka.

(The troika stops and THE OLD MAN gets off.)

Dear God, is there no one in the world I can discuss my agony with? How my son died two weeks ago? How he was my only one, my whole life? How suddenly he's gone, buried and gone?

(The troika keeps going silently.)

SCENE 12

The cabin. Night. THE MEDIC snores in his bed. Enter THE OLD MAN, who shakes him.

OLD MAN: It's me again, do you remember?

MEDIC: How should I remember?

OLD MAN: I came here with my wife a few days ago.

MEDIC: Lots of people have passed through here since.

OLD MAN: It's hard to breathe, my legs are weak, and I'm always thirsty.

MEDIC: Come closer.

(THE OLD MAN sits on a stool in front of THE MEDIC, who examines him.)

Well…Hmmm…Hmmm….Yeaaaaah…

(Pause.)

The flu, or maybe a fever. There's been an outbreak of typhus in the city.

OLD MAN: You told her that too.

MEDIC: Put on a cold compress and take this powder twice a day.

OLD MAN: You gave her that too. And she died.

MEDIC: Well…Yeaaaaah…How old are you?

OLD MAN: Not even seventy-four.

MEDIC: Take it twice a day. *Buonasera.*

OLD MAN: *(To the air.)* From his expression, I knew that circumstances were dire, and that no compress or powder would be of any use. Now it became clear to me that I would be dead soon as well.

(THE OLD MAN faces THE MEDIC. Pause, then, to the air:)

I faced you and looked at you up close, eye to eye, but this time I didn't insist on a bleeding.

MEDIC: What, anything else?

OLD MAN: A question: How is it, doctor, that I know what you're going to say and you know what I'm going to say and we never get an unexpected word between us? Something from the heart?

MEDIC: Yeaaaaah…Something from the heart is a different matter. Something from the heart, a tear in the corner of your eye, for that some conditions must be met. It is a privilege not meant for us. Go home, my friend. I have a lot of people waiting. *Buonasera*

(THE OLD MAN gets up and leaves.)

275

SCENE 13

The main road. Morning. THE OLD MAN.

OLD MAN: While waiting on the main road for the troika to take me back from Khlopka to Pupka, I got lost in thought and began calculating. I realized that death does hold a single benefit: There is no need to eat, nor drink, nor pay taxes or spare the feelings of others. And since you do not lie in death for just a year, but for centuries and millennia, it struck me that death would be highly lucrative. Life is a loss, and death – a net profit. This was undeniably true, but how cruel it is! Why would such a design be instilled in this world, that life is given to man but once, yet it all goes by so pointlessly?

(The troika arrives, in it THE DRIVER and two PROSTITUTES. It stops by THE OLD MAN.)

DRIVER: Back to Pupkah, eh?

OLD MAN: Yes.

(He gets in the troika. It starts moving and the two PROSTITUTES continue their interrupted conversation.)

PROSTITUTE WITH A MOLE: So tell me, those two *pishpushkalach* we met in Schchochi, aren't those the same ones we met in Pjojy?

PROSTITUTE WITH A FRECKLE: The very same.

PROSTITUTE WITH A MOLE: Dear God, the smell! No money…

PROSTITUTE WITH A FRECKLE: No culture…

PROSTITUTE WITH A MOLE: Not much *pishpushkalé* to speak of…

PROSTITUTE WITH A FRECKLE: Once upon a time people were different…Gazapacho De Bello…

PROSTITUTE WITH A MOLE: Where the hell is Gazpacho De Bello? Gone are the days of old!

PROSTITUTE WITH A FRECKLE: Once there was wooing, romance, champagne. Today, they drop their trousers and then – *Pishpushkalé!* A new star is rising in our world – Lord *Pishpushkalé!*

PROSTITUTE WITH A MOLE: Gone are the days of old.

PROSTITUTE WITH A FRECKLE: But just so you know, gentlemen, there are other things in this world. There's heart-*kalé*, there's head-*kalé*, there's humanity-*kalé*, culture-*kalé*, art-*kalé*…There's even theatre-*kalé*, in which an actor-*kalé* stands in a spotlight-*kalé* and delivers a monologue-*kalé*.

PROSTITUTE WITH A MOLE: Oh, what are you babbling about? Even the actor-*kalé* in the middle of his monologue-*kalé* is only thinking about the *pishpushkalé* in the *pushkalé*.

(She recites, as if she were a dramatic actress:)

Oh, *pishpushkalé!*
You shan't rejoice for long in the *pushkalé!*
One day you'll start to shake-*kalé!*
You'll feel a funny ache-*kalé!*
The doc will probe your rump-*kalé!*
He'll find a little lump-*kalé!*
You haven't got a prayer-*kalé!*
You're starting to despair-*kalé!*
You hug your Pop goodbye-*kalé!*
You kiss your Mom and cry-*kalé!*
Then, pow! You're done, that's it-*kalé!*
An end to your bullshit-*kalé!*

(They burst out laughing.)

DRIVER: Still laughing!

OLD MAN: Let them. They don't know yet: In this world, laughter always ends in tears.

DRIVER: If only...

(Pause. The PROSTITUTES fall asleep.)

DRIVER: We've reached Pupkah.

(THE OLD MAN gets off and the troika rides on.)

SCENE 14

(A road in the fields. Night. The PROSTITUTES are asleep and snoring.)

DRIVER: And once again I'm all alone. The sorrow that left me for a little while returns to cruelly crush my heart, so much so that I fear I will no longer be able to bear it. More than two weeks have gone by since he died and I still haven't properly discussed his passing with anybody. The whole thing demands a serious conversation. You have to elaborate solemnly all about how he suddenly got sick, how he suffered, what his last words were, and then eventually how he died. And I have to discuss the funeral. There's so much to say, and whoever's listening will nod their head, give a sigh, maybe even shed a tear or two... Best thing would've been to tell a women. They're dumb, but boy can they cry.

(He stops the troika and gets off.)

DRIVER: On the side of a dirt trail somewhere between Pupkah and Khlopka, or maybe it was Khlopka and Drupkah, or the great road from Schchochi to Pjojy or, perhaps, on some imaginary highway between Paris and Shanghai, I stopped the troika to give rest and food to the horse.

(He feeds the horse and strokes its mane.)

You're chewing with vigor, my friend. Chew away. Since we can't afford barley, you'll have to make due with hay. There's no money, what can I do? I've grown old. My son should have been here in my place. Say, you have big ears and great patience, don't you? You can listen to me. You *understand.* You *know.* You stand there chewing, looking at the world with peaceful brown eyes that see so much. My son died. He was torn away from life. Imagine you had a little kid, a little colt, a horsey. And you love it so, and it's your entire life, and then all of a sudden…

(THE DRIVER buries his face in the horse's neck and cries.)

Oh, my friend. The light of my life, my son died. My only one, barely a boy, got sick all of a sudden and died, never to return. And I loved him so. My life is so empty now. Help me, my friend. Teach me, my horse, teach me how to live from here on out. How to live!

(He stops crying. The horse stops eating. THE DRIVER gets into the troika and drives on.)

SCENE 15

Cabin. Dawn. THE OLD MAN.

OLD MAN: You'd never say to yourself: Something worthwhile is about to happen to this man.

(He lies on the bed.)

All throughout that night images flashed before my eyes: Of our little baby girl, of the willow tree, fish, slaughtered geese, and my old wife, who resembled a bird. Her face, so pale and meek…And all sorts of other faces flew into view and whispered to me about losses and I restlessly tossed and turned in the bed. It was only right before I died that I fell asleep, and for a moment I dreamed: I was seated at the table, balancing my ledger. My old woman was bustling about the cabin.

(He sits and works. THE OLD WOMAN enters and begins tidying up the cabin.)

I stood up from the table.

(He gets up.)

Sit with me, woman.

(THE OLD WOMAN stands, frozen.)

Sit down. We'll eat together. We'll talk.

(She stands frozen. He approaches her and she jerks away.)

What are you afraid of? I'm your husband. I want to sit with you, talk quietly in the candlelight, pleasantly pass the time.

(She stands pressed against the wall.)

And when I reached out my hand to hold you…

(He reaches his hand towards her. She shields her face with her hands.)

What for? I'm not going to hit you. I never did. You were scared for no reason. And I didn't want you to be afraid. I wanted you to feel just once in your heart…just once…

(THE OLD WOMAN chuckles a terrible chuckle, puts her face in her hands, and shrinks into the corner.)

And at the same time I kept seeing another image: What might have been and never was. If things were different, if we had lived differently from the very beginning, why… Joy would have flooded this house. You would have been full of love and, most importantly, you would not have been afraid. And I would have made you laugh.

(They sing and dance.)

And I would have pinched your double chin, like I did with my Mother when I was a little boy.

(He pinches her chin as they dance. She smacks his hand away. They both dance and laugh.)

Let me do it. What do you care? Let me. Oh, I would like to discuss my mother's double chin a little further. Her nipple was another matter altogether, but after that came the double chin. It was very important to me. I want the world to know all about my mother's chin, how I played with it and played with it…I thought I would play forever. And look, what a wonder. My mother's double chin is like sweet bread, and I pinch it and eat it until I'm full for days on end. I pinch it and eat it and it grows back. Think about how much I saved on bread all throughout my life. Seventy years times three hundred and sixty-five. Dear God, what a mother.

(The singing and dancing dies down until they stop altogether.)

But that vision disappeared. It couldn't last. The other image returned, the terrible one from which I could not run.

(THE OLD WOMAN chuckles a terrible chuckle, puts her face in her hands, and shrinks into the corner.)

So I said, 'Why send me this dream? I've suffered enough. We spent our entire life this way. Why remind me of it now and rattle my spirit so?' But a force inside of me, a mocking and ruthless power, would not let me be. Like a scab I couldn't stop picking, I walked back and she rose towards me.

(He stands back. She rises and faces him.)

And once again I reached out my hand, and once again you jolted back and shrunk in fear.

(He reaches out his hand. She jerks back again, shrinks in fear, and puts her face in her hands.)

And then I said, 'Is there no end to this torment?' But soon our motions grew limp, like the dance of two ragdolls.

(They repeat their dance.)

The image faded, losing its color, and grew moldy until it eventually disappeared.

(THE OLD WOMAN disappears and THE OLD MAN lies back in bed.)

But from beneath that image, something else emerged. What was it? It was…

(Enter the three CHERUBS.)

SAD CHERUB: What was it?

HAPPY CHERUB: A noodle?

FUNNY CHERUB: A poodle?

HAPPY CHERUB: Some strudel?

FUNNY CHERUB: A snickerdoodle?

SAD CHERUB: What was it?

OLD MAN: It was that…of which I cannot say a thing.

(He dies.)

END

By the same author

Hanoch Levin: Selected Plays One
Krum / Schitz / The Torments of Job / A Winter Funeral / The Child Dreams
9781786829139

Hanoch Levin: Selected Plays Three
The Thin Soldier / Bachelors and Bachelorettes /
Everyone Wants to Live / The Constant Mourner / The Lamenters
9781786829122

WWW.OBERONBOOKS.COM

Follow us on Twitter @oberonbooks
& Facebook @OberonBooksLondon